PATHWAYS
Models for Composition

Humanities Division — Macon State College

Seventh Edition

PEARSON

Custom
Publishing

PEARSON CUSTOM PUBLISHING
75 Arlington Street, Suite 300, Boston, MA 02116
A Pearson Education Company

This edition of *Pathways* is dedicated to

Mrs. Mary Jo English

who is retiring after thirty-nine years of devoted service
to Macon State College as Senior Secretary
of the Humanities Division.

Foreword

When instructors of freshman English assign certain types of themes, students frequently respond by asking for models. The instructor may point to one or more sample essays in whatever textbook the class uses, but more often than not, these essays are written by professionals; they greatly exceed the shorter lengths of freshman essays, and they may only partially adhere to the guidelines the student has been asked to follow. Yet, freshman composition students, like all other writers, learn best by imitation; they, therefore, need realistic models of the kinds of essays they will be called upon to write.

In *Pathways: Models for Composition*, the Humanities Division of Macon State College addresses this need by providing students and instructors with an anthology of successful essays written by the college's own freshman students. These essays represent those kinds of themes typically assigned by Macon State College instructors in English 1101 and English 1102. Although some of the essays originated as in-class assignments while others were written outside of class, they all reflect the reality of meeting deadlines and the limited revision possible in the face of those constraints. The essays accordingly should stimulate discussion of both the successful strategies students employed to solve composition problems and the alternatives that could have made the essays even stronger.

The publication of these essays will also serve to make students and instructors attentive to the problems of writing for real audiences. When students know that only instructors will read their writing and that the only consequence will be a grade, whether high or low, their essays will likely lack the authentic tone of those who really want to communicate with an audience. By discussing the selections in *Pathways*, however, students will discover that freshman writing generally, and quite possibly their own writing in particular, need not be a mere academic exercise. Moving the emotions of an audience and motivating an audience to share one's viewpoints are compelling and contagious activities. Students who find themselves responding to these essays will know that their own writing possesses a comparable potential, and that knowledge is nothing less than exciting.

The essays in *Pathways* were selected by a committee of the English faculty at Macon State College. It is the Editorial Board's policy to publish the essays as submitted, making only minor corrections. Because the primary objective is to furnish students with a realistic sampling of commonly assigned freshman compositions, the board did not choose some very worthy submissions whose topics and/or formats are less often encountered in freshman English classes.

The Humanities Division frequently publishes a new edition of the anthology, the board wishes to recognize all students who submitted essays for this edition of *Pathways*. Their participation in this project promises to strengthen the writing program at Macon State College, and for that contribution, the Humanities Division expresses heartfelt gratitude.

The Editorial Board
Dr. Debra H. Matthews, Chair
Dr. Amy Berke
Dr. Patrick Brennan
Dr. Sharon Colley

Contents

Argument

Final Exam

English 1102 Models

Fiction

x • Contents

Internationally Local Barriers

Jordan Buecker

Assignment: In this out-of-class essay, the student was to use Anzalduas as a model and write an argument that presents a variety of voices.

According to Charlotte Bronte in *Jane Eyre*, "Prejudices, it is well known, are most difficult to eradicate from the heart whose soil has never been loosened or fertilized by education; they grow there, firm as weeds among stones" ("Quotes for: Prejudice"). Growing up on the island of St. Croix, I was assailed from all sides for many reasons. I endured attacks from the native ethnic group as well as people of my own culture. I was misunderstood and viewed cynically by the locals. At the same time, friends and family residing in the United States attacked my actions and cultural assimilation. There was no acceptable medium that would satisfy both groups while I still lived on the island.

I remember, while still a young boy, walking down the streets of St. Croix I could feel the piercing stares of the natives who thought of Americans as obnoxious, bold, and, beyond our bounds. "Be careful where ya walk, boy!" "Go on to where ya come, mon," "you got no place here, Yankee." For all the effort I put into gaining acceptance, these comments hindered me more than anything. I felt resentment emanating from the locals because I was living on their island, subverting their culture. Some locals were just waiting for a reason to lash out. On one occasion when our family was relaxing, and enjoying a day on the coast, my brother was flying his kite along the beach when he accidentally bumped into a local man. The man immediately exploded and threatened to "cut de boy up" with one of the machetes that were common on the island. It seemed as if he was waiting for any infraction on our part to justify and express his resentment. My attempts to diffuse this cultural resentment were mostly ineffective.

"You are amazing on the steel drums, sir, I would love to learn the instrument." "Ahh, mon, you too white, not enough rhythm for the drums," was the response. *If I couldn't get past these basic discriminations, I certainly would never break through the seemingly insuperable walls of culture.*

I remember people would inquire, asking when my boat got in or when my plane was leaving. "I've lived here for three years; I don't plan on leaving anytime soon," I would say. The stereotype placed on Americans as tourists was a huge impediment to us Americans living on the island on a permanent or semi-permanent basis. I could work side by side with the locals, and the next day my efforts would be forgotten. I remember we were on the island during Hurricane Hugo. My family assisted all the locals that we could before the storm became so fierce that it was lethal to remain outside of a fortified structure. While waiting days for the storm to pass, we helped make sure all was well in the shelter and that everyone was fed and clothed. After the storm had passed, we scoped the island to ascertain the damages. People we passed would ask us, "Didn't get back to your mainland before the storm, ehh?" or say that "ya picked a bad time to visit thee island, Mon." Almost instantly, they had forgotten all of our efforts or were unwilling to recognize our contribution.

My American influence would never disappear. I would always face misunderstandings: "Wat you talkin about?" "Repeat dat," and "Your English make no sense, mon." A linguistic barrier was in place even though both parties spoke English. Until moving to St. Croix, I thought that English was English. *I was terribly mistaken.* I would occasionally be entirely ignored because I couldn't speak "English." *I come from the country where English reigns supreme, and they told me that I could not talk English!* I thought that I could just force my way through this linguistic obstacle and push my dialect on the people. I found that I could push, but all I would be doing was wasting breath. I was not going to be accommodated in any way. I was forced to either forsake certain parts of my identity (my dialect, or perhaps my "Americanism"), or sacrifice communication. At the same time I was trying to break down the cultural walls, I found a simultaneous battle against my friends and relatives living in the United States. Laurence J. Peters states that "against logic, there is no armor like ignorance" ("Quotation #23641 from Michael Moncur").

They had never experienced anything so rich as island life. Yet, they insisted on pushing their ignorance and bigotry. There were comments of disbelief that it is possible to live and function outside of the comfort of the United States: "How can you stand the constant, season-less weather?"

It may be season-less, but it's one, constant, pleasant climate.

"How do you live on such small rations of fresh water?"

How spoiled they were that they took for granted something such as fresh water!

"It must be frustrating to be confined to such a small area!"

"Contained on this tiny space is more diversity than you can imagine!" I would reply. "You need to get back to a civilized life and leave the sticky, troublesome islands to the natives." At that point, I could clearly relate to William Hazlitt's statement that "without the aid of prejudice and custom, I should not be able to find my way across the room" ("Quotes by: Hazlitt, William"). How dare they insult the land that I now adore and tell me what civilized life is supposed to be, having never even thought of leaving their comfortable "bubble"! They thought of the diverse island as little more than a remote vacation spot.

I will never be able to meld completely into any culture other than my own, but through experience, I will know the signs of cultural misunderstanding. I will never be able to fix this cultural fissure without contributions from the other group and further attempts on my part. And, certainly, I will never face any cultural difference from a single angle, but always from multiple angles as different groups in my life interpret my motives and actions differently.

Works Cited

"Quotation #23641 from Michael Moncur." Quotations Page. 1994–2004. Michael Moncur. 6 May 2007 <http://www.quotationspage. com/quote/23641.html>.

"Quotes by: Hazlitt, William." Quotations Book. 2007. 6 May 2007 <http://www.quotationsbook.com/author/3309/page=14>.

"Quotes for: Prejudice." Quotations Book. 2007. 6 May 2007 <http://www.quotationsbook.com/subject/prejudice/>.

A Night to Remember

Marcia Justice

Assignment: In this out-of-class essay, the student was to write a response to a lecture by Lucy Anne Hurston, an event held during the Macon State College Arts Festival.

It's a soft spring twilight. The air is heavy with the thick, sweet smell of wisteria; its lavender vines trellis through the landscape. White cherry blossoms sway gently in the evening breeze. My car windows are down, and I drink in every breath, inhaling the beauty and letting it envelop me. It is a long drive and much traffic. I watch the sun and think of how impossible it is to look directly at its brilliance, even this late in the day. It is beautiful to see the sun's clear silver light playing hide-and-seek through the dense Georgia pines along the highway. I think of how I love its heat: this humid thick Georgia heat. I love its intensity, its ability to bring the earth to life, and the way it changes the air.

There are people, too, who have this gift, this way of changing the very air that we breathe, of infusing it with beauty and possibility. I am on my way this evening to hear a lecture about one of them: Zora Neale Hurston. Her niece, Lucy Anne Hurston, is speaking at the Macon State College auditorium, promoting a book she has produced called *Speak, So You Can Speak Again: The Life of Zora Neale Hurston.* I am excited, anticipatory. I have felt this since I first saw a flyer announcing this Arts Festival event tacked on a hallway bulletin board. I cannot explain this feeling. It is not logical; it does not lend itself to a conscious analysis. I like logic and answers. But in the absence of these, I find that what I do know is that it is the same feeling I most often associate with the way I love music, and having defined it that far, I make a conscious effort to let thought go and simply follow the feeling.

I arrive early. In the lobby of the Arts Complex, the college bookstore has set up a table displaying some of Zora Neale Hurston's best known books. Along side of these is Lucy Anne Hurston's *Speak, So You Can Speak Again*. While purchasing Lucy Hurston's book, I am told that Ms. Hurston will be available to sign it after her presentation. There are a scattering of people already seated as I enter the auditorium. I see Dr. Berke, my English 1102 professor, and her daughter in the last row. I am happy to see her here. She has been an encouragement to me, and her presence immediately quietens the "you- are-so-out-of-place, what-are-you-doing-you-silly-old-woman" demon that has somehow attached itself to me so intensely and so painfully this past year: out-of-place among young college students, out-of-place among higher academia, out-of-place among those with higher literary knowledge. But, I take a deep breath and choose a seat in the middle row to the far outside left. I remove the cellophane covering and begin to explore its contents. I find in the introduction, a quote from "Drenched in Light" that says, "I would like just a little of her sunshine to soak into my soul. I would like that a lot (5)." Hurston's sunshine is wrapped up in this wonderful book with her pictures, poems, plays, and even a CD that allows one to hear her voice, her spirit in the radio interviews, her singing and speaking.

From one of the many envelopes interspersed throughout this remarkable "scrapbook" memoriam to Zora, I pull a tattered brown paper with her poem "Home." It is in old type specific to very old typewriters, the type my grandfather used as a newspaper editor in southwest Florida when he was in his twenties. I used the same type-writer in my long-ago teenage years to write stories and poetry: I recognize the print type, the unique look of how the keys hit the paper. Time slips for a moment, and I think of Zora, sitting at such a typewriter, composing this very poem I am holding in my hand. She is in her moment, involved in her poetry, afterward hand writing "Just a bubbling over of a melancholy heart—momentarily" at the bottom of the page. She has no idea of how valued her work will become or any hint that forty-seven years after her demise, someone will be sitting in an auditorium waiting for her niece to speak about her life.

A woman seated behind me is now looking at the book over my shoulder. "Who exactly is Zora Hurston?" she asks. She explains that she has never heard of Zora and is only attending to earn extra credit for her English class. I begin to show her the book. A few words, and then Lucy Anne Hurston is being introduced and our conversation ceases abruptly. Who, indeed, is Zora Hurston? She is the aunt of Lucy Anne Hurston who is our speaker for the evening. Lucy Hurston herself projects a calm confidence. She is funny and totally charming. Questions, she announces, are welcome at any time during her presentation. She explains that her father was Zora's youngest brother and that he was sixty years old when Lucy was born. She speaks of being a curious nine year old who loved academics and reading. She remembers the exhilaration in learning that she could check books out of the nearby Brooklyn library.

I, too, spent hours in our near-by library in the summertime. It was a small country library in a dilapidated old building with creaky wooden floors, and the smell of musty old books was over-whelming when I opened the massive front doors. It was absolutely one of the most wonderful places in the world, and I cried when it had to be demolished. Lucy Anne Hurston goes on to explain how she developed a system of checking out the maximum five books time and time again until her library privileges were suspended. Unwilling to return the treasured books, nine-year-old Lucy remembers a box in their attic that is full of her father's things. She has seen books in this box. It is a box that she has been told many times that she is not allowed to disturb. She knows, she says, that her "father will beat her" if she bothers this box, but the temptation is too strong. Risking her father's wrath, she climbs to the attic. Here she finds her aunt's book *Their Eyes Were Watching God*. She is cap-tivated immediately. Her nine-year-old self is enthralled, and now she is in a deeper quandary: she has to, has to, HAS TO, ask her father questions, important questions, about her aunt, about this wonderful book, about the rest of the contents of the box. She decides to confess to her father (who does punish her) in order to satisfy her raging curiosity. How unaware she is that this is only the beginning of the intertwining that will occur between her life and and Zora's. Lucy Anne Hurston's favorite book is still *Their Eyes*

Were Watching God. She states that she regards it as the most autobiographical of Zora's works despite the official "autobiography" label attached to *Dust Tracks on a Road*. Ms. Hurston speaks of attending the premier of the movie version of *Their Eyes Were Watching God* with Oprah Winfrey and Hallie Berry.

Lucy Hurston now branches out to discuss Zora herself. She had a sister named Sarah, Lucy says. They were daughters of a Baptist minister in Eatonville, Florida. Eatonville was an extraordinary place by all accounts. In *Speak, So You Can Speak Again*, it states that Eatonville was an all-black town with "little hierarchy of race and class and no segregation or discrimination based on superficial matters such as skin color and hair texture" and that "children were thus allowed to thrive with a sense of pride and security that was denied many black people in the South, and outside of it as well" (10). It is this totally black culture, Professor Hurston remarks, that gave the uniqueness to much of Zora's works. She states that Zora was a free spirit who said, "Here I am" and simply stood by it without apology. Zora Neale Hurston was, in fact, a trained anthropologist who, among many other sterling accomplishments, used her gifts as a writer to record Eatonville's culture and folkways for posterity.

From the audience, a young girl says that her mother is trying to write her life story and asks for Professor Hurston's advice. Professor Hurston tells her that it is important to read and write every day, if only for oneself. She speaks of everyone being special, of everyone having a story within them to tell. I also ask a question about Zora's works and remark that I think Zora is wonderful. I see the look in her eyes before I hear the response. I know this look: it says "you are an older white southern woman. What can you possibly know about the black experience? How can you possibly relate to Zora's works?" Sure enough, I am immediately rebuffed: "She was Brilliant," Professor Hurston states emphatically, a little sharply, emphasizing that "wonderful" did not begin to describe Zora Neale Hurston. She then answers my question graciously but quickly, and moves on.

I want to say that Zora would have understood me. Of this, I am sure. I want to point out the stories about Zora's friendship with Charlotte Mason, at one time also her patron, and a white woman. Even in *Speak, So You Can Speak Again*, they are described as "fast friends who shared a mutual interest in the power of intuition and psychic energy" (20). I think about Lucy Anne Hurston's own words in relaying the following story about Zora as a child: "She would throw up her hand and greet any of the passersbys who struck her fancy and often asked if they'd like for her to walk 'a piece of the way' with them. The answer was usually yes, and so she'd go on a half-mile walk down the road charming them with her curiosity and her stories, then she'd walk back home" (8). I picture Zora meeting me in the road of life and walking "a piece" with me. She, in fact, speaks to many things and many people in both her life and her works. There is no disputing that Zora Neale Hurston is extraordinarily important as a black woman writer, but she transcends these labels and these boundaries, much as she did in life.

Another audience member is now asking if Lucy shares many family traits with Zora. Professor Hurston hesitates. When she answers, it is to say "possibly, maybe. I don't know." It is too much to consider for someone so close to the source. To me, it is clear that Lucy Anne Hurston shines with the same sparkle that her aunt still does through her writings or when we listen to Zora speak and sing on the CD that Lucy plays. The sparkle in Lucy runs out into the audience in waves as she reads an excerpt from one of her own books that describes her father's passing. There is no doubt that she and Zora share kinship, but it is a kinship beyond family blood. The story of her father's passing at ninety-years-old is very moving. Lucy Hurston tries hard to project the words calmly and evenly, but her story and her voice cannot help but communicate the fountains of deep grief, loss, and the bittersweet joys of life that those who have experienced it try so hard to keep contained. She is eloquent. The words are heart-wrenching. She is the girl in pigtails that she describes so well; she is the girl who just wants her daddy back while she plays in the house of her youth. And then, with a sigh, she is a woman again, a professor of a community college, an author, a mother. The story is over.

Professor Hurston wants to "end the evening on an upbeat note," she says, by playing Zora singing a folk song about "Uncle Bud" that was common in juke-joints throughout the South. The song itself garners laughter from the group, as Zora's voice fills the auditorium. When it finishes, Professor Hurston points out that in order to preserve these songs, her aunt had to sing them over and over again to learn them from the individuals she interviewed. At that time, there were no portable electronic devices to record such things. She emphasizes the tenacity and diligence, the passion her aunt devoted to such projects.

Lucy Anne Hurston now says good night to Georgia. She begins to sign books for those who have lined up for her autograph. I watch for a while, thinking of Zora. Finally, I stand in line to have my book signed also. She signs it "For Marcia, Peaceful Regards! Lucy Anne Hurston, March 28, 2007." I am too lucky to have been here tonight in the presence of Lucy Anne Hurston and Zora. I walk out into a balmy spring evening, taking a little of their sunshine with me.

Works Cited

Hurston, Lucy Anne and the Estate of Zora Neale Hurston. "Speak, So You Can Speak Again: The Life of Zora Neale Hurston". Washington, D.C.: Doubleday, 2004.

A Great Destination

James Franklin

Assignment: In this out-of-class essay, the student was to develop a descriptive essay.

Although there are many places across this great country in which to vacation, the Gulf Coast, Orlando, and Las Vegas are often favorites. Other locations visited by millions of people every year are Yosemite National Park, Niagara Falls, and Washington, D.C. Every single one of these places is a superb choice for a vacation, if one enjoys crowds, heavy traffic and expensive hotel rooms. However, the Colorado Rocky Mountains, my favorite vacation destination, offers remarkable landscapes, diverse wildlife, and an abundance of solitude. I have had the good fortune of vacationing in the Colorado Rocky Mountains not only once, but twice.

The beautiful sights from the peaks of the Colorado Rocky Mountains can be awe inspiring. As one looks down into the valleys, the vibrant color of the leaves seems to dance in the wind. The golden yellow of the aspen leaves, the dark green needles of the spruce, and the reds and tans of the hardwoods all seem to come to life with the slightest breeze. If someone looks closely into this magnificent palette of color, he or she may see a stream with clear sparkling mountain water cascading down into the valley. A soothing sound catches the ear as the water glides over and around numerous rocks. The music of the water can erase the worries of everyday life, if only for a short while. Still enjoying the rainbow of color and the soothing sound of water, one should be on the lookout for Colorado's most famous animal, the elk.

The Colorado Rocky Mountains is the premiere place in the country to see the majestic elk. A large mature bull elk can weigh as much as seven hundred pounds and have antlers that measure five feet across; even so, the elk is a very difficult animal to see in the wild. The elusiveness of the elk adds to the excitement of seeing one in the wild. If one sees an elk or hears the bugle of a bull during the rut, the experience will last a lifetime. Black bear and mule deer also reside within the mountains of Colorado. The bear population, in fact, is so great that one has to be vigilant so as not to be attacked. This possibility of attack, in itself can lead to a memorable vacation. Another animal popular in Colorado is the mule deer. The population has been on the decline in recent years, but there are sufficient numbers to make seeing a mule deer very possible. With the population decline, the mule deer grow larger antlers, which make seeing one even more enjoyable. Although one is not guaranteed an opportunity to see one of Colorado's famous animals, one can be guaranteed a peaceful and solitary vacation.

The Colorado Rocky Mountains contain some of the remotest areas in the continental United States. Some of these areas, classified as wilderness areas, are only open to horse or foot travel and closed to vehicular traffic at all times. If someone wishes solitude and is willing to put forth the effort, these areas are just the place to go on a vacation, but getting to these wilderness areas is not easy. The terrain is very rugged, with steep peaks and deep valleys. Not only is the terrain rugged, but one has to deal with the altitude as well, with some peaks reaching as high as fifteen thousand feet. If someone is not in excellent physical condition, then the wilderness areas may not be the place to go. Vehicles easily reach much of Colorado, and during certain times of the year, even the areas with easier access can offer a peaceful and relaxing vacation.

Even though the mountains are rugged, they are very appealing. With the cold mountain streams of summer, the colorful leaves of autumn, and the snow capped peaks of winter, the Colorado Rocky Mountains is a good choice for a vacation, any time of the year. Everyone can enjoy the Colorado Rocky Mountains. While only the physically fit should attempt to visit the wilderness areas, the other areas of Colorado offer a great vacation also. The remarkable landscapes, diverse wildlife, and the solitude of the Colorado Rocky Mountains make this area of the country a great vacation destination.

A Daughter's Influence

Donna Jarvis

Assignment: In this out-of-class assignment, the student was to write an essay about an important lesson that she has learned or about someone who has had a positive influence on her life.

I can clearly recall the question my seven-year-old daughter asked me four years ago, "Mama, why are you still with my daddy when he treats you so mean?" Panic seized control of my body when I realized my supposed secret was not a secret after all. She knew I was being abused! Even though she did not realize it at the time, my daughter became the person who had the most positive influence in my life. She opened the door which allowed me to make decisions that changed our lives for the better.

After realizing my daughter knew about the abuse, I knew that I had to make decisions that would eventually affect all of us. I had to decide whether to stay with my husband or leave him. I had convinced myself to stay in my marriage because I believed my children needed to be reared by two parents. Since the abuse was not hidden, I had to ask myself if I wanted my children brought up in an unhealthy environment. Due to my unhappiness, I could not interact with my children. My children needed a mother who could be there for them and do things with them; I was not that mother. I could not even give my daughter the attention she so desperately craved because I was too afraid of my husband; he wanted all of my attention. Therefore, she did not get the nurturing she needed from me. There were many questions I had to ask myself, and knowing that my daughter knew about the abuse helped me to make my decision to leave.

Soon after I left my husband, I went to an attorney and filed for divorce. Afterwards, I felt a peace wash over my entire body, and I knew I was doing the right thing. My children could already tell a difference in me; I could tell a difference in my children. We were happier. Unfortunately, the divorce was not finalized because my husband chose to take his own life. This tragic, self-ish act forced me into making even more decisions about our lives. Instead of rearing my children with the stigma attached to being a divorcee, I was now facing an entirely different situation as a widow. Before I left my husband, we did not function together as a family. However, this tragedy allowed my children and me to mourn together, thereby pulling us together as a family. I found myself being their mother, father, protector, provider, and chief disciplinarian. Whoever said being a single mother was easy was totally wrong. It was a challenging job, one of the most exhaust-ing jobs I have ever had, but I enjoyed every minute of it. I had no regrets about the decisions I made. I found strength deep inside myself that I never knew existed. Before leaving my husband, my daughter and I had lost that bond we developed after she was born, but now we found ourselves bonding once again. I was able to give the nurturing and attention to her that she rightly deserved. It turned out that leaving was the right decision.

Three years after adjusting to everything and having time to heal, our lives changed once again. The love of my life walked right into my life. After our first date, I invited him to my home in order for him to meet my children because they would be involved in any relationship I chose to build. Being able to commit to a rela-tionship with this man was another decision I had to make. Should I become totally involved with this man? Should I let him get close to my children? I considered everything and felt he was the best thing that had ever happened to my children and me. I decided he was the man for all of us. It was nice having someone I did not have to worry about abusing me; therefore, it was easy for my children to accept him. However, my daughter's acceptance of him came gradually. Her final acceptance came once she saw that I was happy and that my relationship with him did not sever the bond she and I had developed together. In fact, the relationship between my daughter and me grew stronger and continues to grow stronger every day. She and I are now closer than ever before. I eventually married this wonderful man, and he legally adopted my children. He became the husband I deserved and the father I always wanted for my children. Marrying him was my best decision yet.

Thinking back to that day four years ago when my daughter asked me her question, I can now smile. On that day, my children's lives and mine changed for the better. It caused me to step back and examine my life, therefore enabling me to make life-changing decisions. When my daughter is older, I will let her know just how much of an influence she had on her mother.

Goodbye

Evelyn Castro

Assignment: In this in-class essay, the student was to narrate a significant event in her life.

"Why are you doing this to me? Don't you love me any more? Don't you care?" I shouted at my mother in rage.

"Of course I still care! But I have to leave, sweetie. There are a lot of things I have to sort out. It's not your fault, Evelyna. Please don't ever think it was your fault."

"I hate you!" I screamed and ran to my room, slamming the door behind me.

The school bus dropped me off a block from my house that Tuesday, and I walked the remaining distance home in the sticky heat of June. The air felt very thick, and I heard the locusts chattering loudly in the trees. As I neared my house, I saw my mom's dark blue Blazer parked in the driveway. I noticed how dirty it was and how much junk was piled up inside. My mom's Golden Retriever, Cleo, lay panting in the shade of the truck. I grabbed the knob to the front door and pushed it open, letting the screen door slam behind me.

The house felt deliciously cold as I stepped inside and put down my books. I smelled the aroma of fresh brewed coffee coming from the kitchen and noticed many of my mother's belongings on the sewing table. Lying on the table was a dirty, square, glass ashtray with a burning cigarette resting in one corner. My mother's cream and silver Zippo lighter engraved with her initials was not far from the ashtray. A half-empty Benson and Hedges cigarette pack, which appeared to have been crushed in my mother's front pocket, lay adjacent to her black and white coffee cup. The cup had drops of coffee running down the outside and had no doubt made a ring on the sewing table. A pile of my mother's clothes, containing several unfolded shirts and jeans, had been placed next to a black suitcase on the floor.

Wondering why the suitcase and clothes were there, I walked down the hall to my parents' room, brushing by the chair in front of the sewing table as I did. The chair had a hideous orange and brown seat back that was worn and frayed from age. As I walked down the hall, I detected both the pleasant aroma of cinnamon potpourri and the pungent odor of feline urine coming from the litterbox in the bathroom. I noticed how the shades, having been let up, allowed enough sun to shine through and reveal just how dirty the floors were. As I neared my parents' room, I faintly heard the radio playing a song from Yanni's *Live from the Acropolis.* The door to their room was partially open.

Looking inside, I could see that the bed was unmade, and a small suitcase half full of my mother's clothes was lying on it. I opened the door the rest of the way and observed my mom hustling around the room opening and closing drawers and closets. I noticed how her wire-rimmed glasses kept sliding down her nose as she went about the room. Every few seconds she would pause and push the glasses back up to where they belonged.

"What are you doing?" I suddenly asked, startling her as I did. I heard the ceiling fan clicking and whirring as she hesitated to answer.

"I'm packing," she finally replied.

"Why?" I inquired.

"I have to leave, Evelyna. I can't live here anymore." She was addressing me by my real name, the one I went by at the time.

"Yes, you can." I retorted. "You just don't want to!"

"Honey, it's not like that. It's just—Damn it! You're too young to understand!" She grabbed her suitcase from the bed and started down the hall. I followed her to the sewing table and watched as she gathered clothes from the pile on the floor and crammed them into the half-full suitcase.

"I'm not too young! Why don't you try to explain it to me? I deserve an explanation!" My mother sat down in the chair by the sewing table and lit a cigarette. Her glasses slid down her nose, as they always did, and she pushed them back up. She drew in a puff of smoke and then exhaled slowly, calming herself as she did.

"Evelyna, I have to start over and find myself. I started too young. It's not your fault; it's just something that happens. You can come with me if you like. I want you to be with me."

"Why are you doing this to me? Don't you love me anymore? Don't you care?" I shouted at my mother in rage.

"Of course I still care! But I have to leave, sweetie. There are a lot of things I have to sort out. It's not your fault, Evelyna. Please, don't ever think it was your fault." She was pleading, but I ignored it.

"Don't call me Evelyna! I hate that name!" I didn't really hate the name, but she had given it to me and I knew my words would hurt her. I saw an expression of pain come across her face.

"Sweetie, please don't do—"

"I hate you!" I screamed and ran to my room, slamming the door behind me. Within a few minutes my mother was knocking on my door asking to be let in. She told me that she wanted to talk and say goodbye. I heard her crying as she stood at my door knocking. I felt so terrible about ignoring her. I wanted to make her feel better, but I also wanted her to feel my pain and anger. The knocking and pleading ceased, and minutes later I heard the Blazer door slam. I glanced out the window momentarily and saw mascara and tears streaming down my mother's face. Cleo barked out the truck window as it backed out of the driveway. My mom drove off, and within seconds the loud motor of the Blazer became a hum and then a faint whisper.

The Role of Gender in Mr. & Mrs. Smith

Chanteria Davis

Assignment: Select a film, and using comparison and contrast, analyze how the film in some ways affirms and in other ways challenges our culture's gender norms.

Gender has been one of the most talked about topics in today's society. Many of the things that individuals participate in revolve around gender. Today, men and women still seem to carry gender stereotypes into their personal lives, their beliefs, and their work. The movie *Mr. & Mrs. Smith*, starring Angelina Jolie and Brad Pitt, is about a man and a woman who find themselves in a peculiar situation that leads to love at first sight. The couple eventually marries, but fails to tell each other about their secret lives. Ultimately, the two discover that they are both assassins working for enemy companies. The lead characters of *Mr. & Mrs. Smith* at times affirm and at other times challenge our culture's beliefs about gender.

Jane Smith presents herself like any other woman of the twenty-first century. Mrs. Smith is very intelligent and hard working. She exudes beauty and femininity in every sense of the word. Jane believes in maintaining a career, a marriage, and a home. She also believes that a woman should be independent and is capable of doing the same job as any man. These aspects of her personality affirm our culture's belief about how women should act, look, and think. Jane embodies this ideal woman in a scene from the movie that shows her at home fulfilling domestic and wifely duties, such as cooking, cleaning, and rearranging the furniture.

Although Jane's character represents most women of today, she does display some characteristics that challenge our culture's belief about the role of women. In her line of work, Jane's job is to assassinate enemies on her company's hit list. Women today are not expected to be involved in combat and killing. Also, most women are not expected to have such extravagant shooting and knife handling skills. Women who handle guns and knives are generally seen as being masculine. Jane Smith's character is clearly the opposite of that stereotype.

John Smith, on the other hand, is a typical male of the twenty-first century. He is a very handsome man with a muscular physique. He is a hard working man who is devoted to his marriage and his personal beliefs. John also enjoys playing manly sports such as boxing, poker, football, and gun shooting. John Smith represents sexuality, masculinity and sincerity. He often wears his heart on his sleeve. John shows these traits in the movie when he comes home after a hard day of work, greets his wife lovingly, and sits down at dinner to discuss her feelings and her day. John's actions in this scene affirm our culture's beliefs about the abilities, characteristics, and habits of the ideal male.

Even though John is a masculine guy, he, too, harbors certain traits that make him different from most males in today's society. John Smith possesses a sensitive side that most males would hide. This can be seen when John spends the night with his friend. He is lying on the couch thinking about how he will handle the discovery that his wife is his professional enemy. His friend advises him to kill Jane, but John does not want to because he loves her. In the scene, John seems to be crying. Society generally frowns upon men who show such sensitivity. Most men feel that showing any kind of emotion is a sign of weakness. Here John's actions challenge the masculine stereotype.

These characters both affirm and challenge society's beliefs on gender. John and Jane Smith are able to maintain the stereotypical norms of their genders, such as their appearance, beliefs, and over all love for one another. Still, the couple also shows that men and women can live outside of their gender stereotypes and still preserve a healthy marriage. Jane shows that a woman can be smart, sexy, and feminine, while working in a dangerous field. John shows that a man can be masculine and still possess a hint of sensitivity. In all, society has set opinions about how males and females should act and interact. The protagonists of *Mr. & Mrs. Smith* affirm some of these beliefs through their marriage roles, but participate in other activities that defy gender stereotypes.

Works Cited

Mr. & Mrs. Smith. Dir. Doug Liman. Perf. Brad Pitt and Angelina Jolie. 20th Century Fox, 2005.

Jimi and Charlie

Doug Furney

Assignment: In this in-class essay, the student was to compare two persons, places, or events.

In the late 1960's Jimi Hendrix, a phenomenal young black guitarist, burst onto the expanding music scene of the time. He was considered a flamboyant wild man who created extravagant sonic explosions with his guitar. Almost two decades earlier, Charlie Parker re-defined jazz music. Parker created a revolution with his spectacular saxophone playing. Following in the footsteps of Louis Armstrong, Parker ordained his own unique style which came to be known, among jazz circles, as "bebop." Jimi Hendrix and Charlie Parker became legends, and they remain legends long after their deaths. Like all legends, their lives are shrouded in myths and lore; yet Hendrix and Parker left behind a legacy of American music. Their music shows the emotion, inspiration, and genius of two tragic giants of American cultural art.

The music of Hendrix and Parker touches the soul. Their emotions and musical virtuosity are sometimes so complex and involved that their music is difficult to listen to, but it is always appealing. Both men were, at the beginnings of their careers, not fully recognized and appreciated in America, so they first became well-known in Europe. Hendrix was given his initial chance to shine in London, and Parker first became renowned in Paris. Both men were masters of their instruments. Hendrix created art through the technological manipulation of the electric guitar. Hendrix physically and artistically violated the instrument, producing sounds only his mind had ever imagined. Parker, similarly, demonstrated his technique acoustically with the saxophone. Like Hendrix, Parker ravished his instrument and made music that only he dreamed of. In the scheme of music history, Hendrix and Parker are not regarded as serious or exceptional composers, but in a century, they will likely be remembered as two of America's best music makers. Hendrix created a wide variety of music that ranged from old Southern blues to avant-garde jazz. His influences came from all types of American music. Hendrix directly or indirectly drew from Robert Johnson, James Brown, and Bob Dylan, who created musical revolutions of their own. Charles Parker, nonetheless, drew upon virtually no influences when creating music. He rejected the dixieland and swing jazz of his era and came up with something more complete and brilliant. Parker wrote music for orchestra as well as for small jazz ensembles. Parker's range of composition took him from majestic concert halls in Paris to ragged dance hall barns in rural America. Both men's music remains astonishingly fresh. Their music is timeless and gives America world-wide cultural significance.

All musicians and lovers of music gain from the legacy of Hendrix and Parker. Their legacy made new ideas more acceptable; they dignified art over commercial and popular success, and, most importantly, they gave America a real musical heritage. The changes they made were revolutionary and irreversible. No longer do people look at a guitar or saxophone the same way after experiencing the sounds of Hendrix or Parker. No longer does music sound the same. Hendrix's hands dwarfed his guitar, and he played so seemingly effortlessly that the Fender Stratocaster guitar he played seemed like an extension of his body. His emotions flowed from every string he touched. Parker's saxophone playing is equally as vibrant as Hendrix's guitar playing. Parker's solos were so brazenly unique that his solos set a precedent by taking on their own melodies, rhythms, and harmonies. His verve and emotions showed every time his lips touched his sparkling gold saxophone. Hendrix and Parker have inspired countless musicians and devoted fans. Hendrix, without a doubt, inspired and influenced every guitarist who ever heard him play. Not only rock guitarists, but jazz players as well, regard Hendrix as someone amazingly talented. Virtuosos like John McLaughlin, Eddie Van Halen, and Vernon Reid admit that Hendrix stands alone as a guitar god. Parker, like Hendrix, created music so unique that every type of musician can gain from his body of work; even Hendrix tried to get Parker's saxophone tone on his guitar. Miles Davis, John Coltrane, and Branford Marsalis are deeply indebted to the genius of Charlie Parker. Despite Hendrix and Parker's success, there are no street signs, statues, music halls, or monuments honoring them; yet, their legacy touches all who listen to any form of modern American music. Heavy metal, rap, fusion, and jazz traditionalists borrow or copy directly from the music of Jimi Hendrix and Charlie Parker.

Hendrix and Parker's lives both ended in tragedy before either man had perfected his art. Hendrix got caught up in the excessive drug culture of the 1960's, but his use of drugs is widely exaggerated. Hendrix was not a drug addict, as confirmed by his autopsy, but drugs spurred his untimely death. A fatal dose of barbiturates killed him at the age of twenty-seven. In like manner, drugs and alcohol abuse brought the life of Charlie Parker to an end. Near the end of his life, Parker was known as something of a "junkie-king" among the jazz world. Parker's addiction to heroin lost him many jobs and much money. Parker's heavy drinking complicated his serious problem with stomach ulcers. While visiting a friend in New York in 1955, he died only a few months before his thirty-fifth birthday. Although both men's lives ended tragically, every time their music is played, they live, for a moment, again. Their art triumphed over their short lives, and nobody since has captured the spirit of their art—the emotion, inspiration, or genius.

From the smoke-filled Storyville jazz club in 1952 to the thousands of psychedelic-induced hippies at Woodstock in 1969, Jimi Hendrix and Charlie Parker practiced and created their art. They are shapers of American music whose lives ended in tragedy, but their music transcends their tragic deaths. Their music is what they will ultimately be remembered for. They are visionaries, showing people what music can and should be; they are truly the Beethoven and Mozart of America.

Two Perspectives on the AIDS Epidemic

Era Singh

Assignment: In this out-of-class essay, the student was to compare and contrast two articles, one from a U.S. publication and one from a foreign publication, on the same subject.

Acquired Immune Deficiency Syndrome (AIDS) is a dreaded disease that has affected the lives of many throughout the world. It has taken on distinct characteristics and patterns in each country. In Steven Findlay's "AIDS: The Second Decade," Findlay clearly describes the origins of AIDS in the United States. In "150,000 Sex Workers in India HIV-infected," Arvind Kala outlines the contrasting origins of AIDS in India. Both articles explain the reactions of the government and people in their respective countries. The only similarity between the situations in the U.S. and India is that AIDS has reached epidemic proportions in both countries. From these two articles, each country's distinct and different attitudes on AIDS become evident.

Findlay begins his article by describing the first cases of AIDS in the United States. Over ten years ago in Los Angeles, five young homosexual men died from a mysterious collapse of their immune systems. The Center for Disease Control nicknamed the condition Gay Related Immune Deficiency (GRID). Soon the disease struck heterosexuals, and researchers switched to the term AIDS.

"The outcasts of society—gay men, intravenous drug abusers, impoverished blacks, and Hispanics"—were hit the hardest, according to Findlay (20). The beginnings of AIDS in India are quite different. Kala reports that the first diagnosed cases of AIDS appeared only recently. Following the African pattern, India's origins began in the heterosexual community. Then prostitutes spread the disease through their clients (20).

The longevity of the disease in each country has affected the people's reactions toward it. Since AIDS has been publicized for many years, Findlay presents a positive outlook on the treatment of AIDS-related issues. He recalls the 1985 death of movie star Rock Hudson which made AIDS seem less remote. Throughout the nation, support groups sprang up, and new sympathy developed for AIDS patients. The government began to fund AIDS research and pass laws to protect the rights of AIDS patients. After pressure from the public, the government also took an active role in educating Americans about AIDS. The Attorney General advocated "safe sex" and supported HIV/AIDS education in public schools. On the other hand, AIDS is relatively new in India. Kala found that the majority of India's population, including health care workers, were unaware of the ways the disease is spread. An Indian diagnosed with AIDS is an outcast with no place to turn. Even the government cannot help the situation. Kala says the corruption and sheer poverty of the government prevent it from educating the millions of people in India. In addition, there is no information on the status of AIDS in rural areas.

Findlay and Kala agree on only one aspect of AIDS. It is an epidemic. In the United States, a projected 500,000 people will die while an estimated 1.5 million are infected with the disease. AIDS has spread to all levels of society and is said to be nondiscriminatory. Within the next decade, researchers predict that every U.S. resident will be touched by AIDS (Findlay 22). The outlook is just as grim in India. An assessment by the government states that 637,000 people in urban areas are infected (Kala 20). Although AIDS was brought to India only a few years ago, Kala reports that it has already reached the third and final stage of an epidemic. In this third stage, the disease reaches the general population.

In Findlay's and Kala's articles, contrasting attitudes towards AIDS are conveyed. Findlay discusses AIDS as a familiar issue and mentions events expecting the reader to recall them. He champions the steps made toward understanding AIDS by the government and the public. He gives the impression that the familiarity of the U.S. with AIDS has bred greater broadmindedness toward individuals in high risk groups such as homosexuals. After a decade, the public is able to accept the disease and is now trying to stop it from spreading and stop the pain it has caused. India is not as progressive. With great concern, Kala reveals the ignorance of many in regard to AIDS. AIDS has not become common knowledge yet and is a source of confusion for most. Although the government does see AIDS as a major problem, it cannot reach many people. Kala sadly reports India's helplessness toward the threat of AIDS.

AIDS is a dreadful disease that has invaded both the U.S. and India. It has affected the U.S. since the early 1980's while India is still overcoming its initial shock. In the U.S., people have rallied together to raise AIDS awareness and deal with the disease. Unfortunately, India has not taken any visible actions toward educating the public or preventing AIDS from spreading. Thus, the only element common to the two articles is that AIDS has infected the general population in both countries to epidemic proportions. The U.S. has reacted to AIDS with compassion and has tried to combat spreading. In contrast, India stands with her hands tied as a disease overwhelms her.

Works Cited

Findlay, Steven. "AIDS: The Second Decade." *U.S. News and World Report.* 17 June 1991: 20–22.

Kala, Arvind. "150,000 Sex Workers in India HIV-infected." *News India.* 22 Jan. 1993: 20.

The Impact of Technology: The Performing Arts

Christy C. Shannon

Assignment: In this out-of-class essay, the student was asked to write a causal analysis examining the impact of technology on some aspect of today's world.

Titanic, Showboat, Ragtime. What do all of these Tony Award-winning Broadway musicals have in common? All rely heavily on the use of technology for a successful performance. Gone are the days when the curtain must be closed before each set changes in order for stagehands dressed in black to draw weighty sets onto the stage. Now, with the press of a button, ships sink, sets rotate, or stage floors revolve. Various aspects of many theatrical productions depend upon computers. Examples include tickets sold through the Internet, lighting and audio cues programmed into a computer, and the movement of sets controlled by computer. Indeed, the impact of technology on the performing arts, specifically theatre and dance, has thus far been immense. Thanks to the Internet, actors, dancers, instructors, directors, choreographers, and technicians have a plethora of resources to use, and gadgets such as compact disc recorders for personal computers are making the huge task of putting on a show a little more manageable. Even computerized lighting boards are relatively simple to learn to use and certainly leave little margin for error during a performance. Undoubtedly the effect of technology on the arts has been positive, but has there not also been some negative impact? What do performers and others involved in theatre and dance have to gain from technology as compared to what they have to lose?

Without a doubt, the Internet provides immeasurable resources to dance and theatre instructors. A worn-out dance teacher can go to Tapdance.com, for instance, and find some refreshing and new choreography to add pizzazz to a warm-up or routine. While this convenience does eliminate an element of original choreography, the need for time and money spent to attend dance conventions is also eliminated. Theatre instructors can enjoy parallel benefits. Are the same old improvisation exercises becoming dull in class? One can simply log on to "The Improv Homepage" where fresh ideas abound. Theatrical directors are able to peruse and order scripts on the Internet. Equally, dance instructors can examine and order costumes. In all, technology—namely, the Internet— appears to be of great use to dance and drama teachers.

Similarly, students have resources available to them from the Internet. Live demonstrations of ballet terms are available, and dancers trying to learn all of their tap steps can visit the previously mentioned website—Tapdance.com—for a list of basic tap terms and definitions. Theatre and dance students alike can make use of invaluable audition and schooling information. Many web sites related to theatre and dance contain this useful information and so much more.

As stated earlier, new computers and gadgets are making the task of putting together a production a little lighter. Whether the production is a one-act play, a dance recital, or a Tony Award-winning musical, computers aid the production staff. And while costly at first, these items will cut costs in the long run. Foremost, the use of computerized lighting, sound, and sets certainly makes for a smoother, indeed better, show. A better show will almost inevitably sell more tickets, thus making the show more profitable. Second, if dance teachers are able to record their performance music onto a compact disc by purchasing a piece of hardware for their personal computers, they no longer have to spend hundreds of dollars paying someone else to do it for them. Finally, a theatre can certainly save money by having the box office open less often. Keeping fewer hours at the box office is becoming possible by the increasing number of audience members buying tickets over the Internet.

What about the audience? Is the Internet strictly a way to purchase tickets to shows quickly and easily (without having to wait in line), or can the audience enjoy further benefits from it as well? Updated show information such as cast changes, cancellations, and a show's libretto, to name a few, are available at an individual show's websites or at Broadway.Com. With such an intimate feeling of really knowing what is happening with a given production, surely audiences cannot resist buying souvenirs over the Internet, contributing once again to the profit of a given production.

With so many people in performing arts benefiting from the impact of technology, are there other people in the same field who are not? One might consider for a moment technology's impact on education. Theatre classes are being traded for computer classes, music stands are traded for computers, and the only humming to be heard at school is that of a computer being turned on. Does this kind of impact lessen the positive things gained by technology? Probably not yet. However, if children whose only exposure to the arts is at school are no longer given the opportunity to develop, or even discover, their talent, someday in the future the negative effects will resound.

Without a doubt, advances in technology have made a superior impact on performing arts. The Internet, various computers, and new hardware for personal computers will continue to benefit the arts in the future, but only if there are performers to watch, directors to organize, and technicians to run the show. One hopes that those who are given the enormous task of deciding what the children of America should be learning will recognize how well technology and the arts work together and educate children accordingly.

Works Cited

"Tap Dance Homepage." 18. Sep. 2000. <http://www.tapdance.org>

"The Improv Page." 18 Sep. 2000. <http://improvcomedy.com>

Leibovitz at the High

Paul O'Dea

Assignment: In this out-of-class essay, the student was to evaluate the subject of his choice.

This past November, I got the chance to attend the Annie Leibovitz exhibit of photography at Atlanta's High Museum of Art. When I arrived, I was overwhelmed by the hundreds of people waiting in line, and I knew I was in for a special experience. In her show, Ms. Leibovitz uses both color and monochrome (sometimes referred to as black and white) photographs, as well as a magnetic resonance image (MRI). She has an uncommon talent in her use of color, light, and perspective—employing all of these in her pictures of famous and beloved people. Her intent is obviously to photograph her subjects in a way that will show their true character. In every case, she brings these celebrities to a place where we can appreciate them as real people and not as untouchable idols.

Some visitors to the exhibit didn't like the way her work was displayed, but I could see no better way to view Ms. Leibovitz's art than the way she does. She presents her small, original photos, mounted only on simple matting, with none of the distractions of fancy frames or decoration. Describing a few pieces that move me the most will give an impression of what Ms. Leibovitz is trying to say through her art.

The first sequence of photos to catch my eye was of the Rolling Stones' 1975 World Tour. In this set, Ms. Leibovitz is trying to catch what the life of a rock star is like. In monochrome, she shows the great admiration of the crowds that came to see the band in her picture *Fans at the Fence*, Rich Stadium, California. She moves on to present the reclusion that goes with fame in a photo of Keith Richards and son, attempting to enjoy a quiet moment together on the road by setting up a model race track on a hotel bed. The most poignant image in this series is that of Mick Jagger's forearm, just prior to the removal of huge stitches from his wrist following a suicide attempt. I came back to this photo several times to see and hear the passing crowd's reactions and found them much the same each time—a blend of gruesome disgust and heartfelt sympathy for Mick. This image is an enlightening statement of what the pressures of fame can lead to.

Ms. Leibovitz carries her insightful view of the common man in monochrome to her witness of *Christmas at Soledad Prison*, California. From right to left, viewers are told the story in pictures of this trying day: the anxious wait of loved ones outside, the tender greetings, serious conversations, and emotional good-byes. The subjects seem to be asking that their pain be recorded on film. This series works powerfully to bring to light the anxiety of imprisonment on both the convicts and their families—a very thought-provoking account. A perfect example of Annie Leibovitz's ability to capture true character is in the wonderful photograph of Whoopi Goldberg. Here she does a remarkable job of putting Whoopi's well-known personality on film. In this color picture, Ms. Leibovitz is shooting straight down on Ms. Goldberg in a white porcelain tub filled with white milk. Ms. Goldberg's arms, legs, and face are all that pierce the surface, reaching up toward the camera. Her smile is of such giddy humor; no one could mistake that Ms. Leibovitz has caught the contented power Whoopi has in her personal life and career. It's almost as if Whoopi is making a statement of her capacity to rise out of a white world, while loving every second of it.

The technical and artistic gifts possessed by this artist are best demonstrated in her composition of John Cleese, suspended upside down in a tree. Mr. Cleese is dressed in a black body suit that exposes only his feet, hands, and face. His feet are just touching the bottom of a limb—like a bat against the approaching twilight sky. The potential for action is definitely implied; the viewer almost expects John to flap his arms and fly off into the darkness. This whole image has a playful, yet eerie, effect. Ms. Leibovitz's use of the little available light works well to illuminate her subject against that gorgeous sky.

A real departure from the bulk of the exhibition, and the least understood, was a string of MRI scans of Laurie Anderson's head. This set of images goes from the right wall of her skull and progresses in layers (sixteen in all) to the outer left ear. I'm not sure that the intent was here, but I did find it fascinating because I had never seen an MRI before. To present an MRI scan of a famous person could be an assertion of all man's humility and openness.

Ms. Leibovitz continued to surprise us with her imagination and versatility. In an underwater photograph of diver Greg Louganis, she froze him in motion in a way that made one wonder if he was in or out of the water. It took a closer look to find the tiny bubbles created by Greg's breath as he reaches the depth of the descent. The lighting in this photo is so convincing that, until I noticed the bubbles, I simply accepted the walls of the pool as an overcast sky.

The final photograph I viewed, that of Jodie Foster, was my pick for best use of color and light. Ms. Foster has never looked better. She is poised in the surf wearing a lovely red evening gown just as the sun has set behind her. The colors of the sky and the texture of the water alone create a beautiful portrait of nature, but again, Ms. Leibovitz maximizes her use of this colorful light by reflecting it onto Jodie, making the entire composition carry that same natural quality. It's amazing how Leibovitz's use of light works to give an incredible three-dimensional effect to a piece on an otherwise flat media.

I have always been a lover of beautiful photography, and there was no shortage of that at this show. Annie Leibovitz takes her craft far beyond mere beauty. The ability she has to capture one's persona is overshadowed only by her gift of finding it in the first place. That is why so many celebrities request her whenever their portrait is needed. The number of famous people she has had the opportunity to photograph in her young life is an achievement in itself. Her art brings out the true feelings in people, whether they are happy, sad, or terrifying. I'm glad I had this occasion to see more of her work, and I encourage everyone to do the same the next time her exhibit is in town.

Should Mom and Dad Allow You to Buy Sugar?

Christy C. Shannon

Assignment: In this out-of-class assignment, the student was asked to analyze a visual text and explain the values or ideals conveyed in the text.

Picture for a moment a young girl, perhaps eleven or twelve years old, standing in the magazine aisle at the drug store. What does she look like? Is she short or tall? Is she thin or chunky? Is her appearance neat or a little disheveled? Does what she wants to look like have a connection to her reaching for a copy of *Sugar*, Britain's version of *Seventeen* magazine? Perhaps it is possible that fears of being unfashionable or too fat have not taken over her thoughts yet, and she chooses *Sugar* because the cover is splashed with her favorite color—hot pink. Or maybe she is simply enamored with the sound of a British accent, and "Britain's best selling girls' magazine" scrawled across the top of the cover catches her attention. Whatever the reason for initially choosing *Sugar*, or another magazine similar to it, the effect it has on her will be long lasting.

The bright yellow and hot pink writing against a light blue background may catch the child's eye, but the image of a young, probably anorexic or bulimic, certainly airbrushed, model on the cover will stay with her. Indeed, the editors feel so greatly the need to focus on the model that they partially hide with her head the title of the magazine. The young girl holding the magazine is probably already thinking of how she hopes to look like "that" in a couple of years. Of course, the very next image to captivate the girl is found about two-thirds of the way down the page. The bright yellow, all-capitalized print stating, "Boys, boys, boys," accompanied by three subtitles guaranteeing "boy magnetism" and "himtuition," most likely have her in awe. To the right, the hot pink circle with yellow writing promises a poster special of New York's "hottest hunks." Is she now envisioning a fond farewell to the teddy bear pictures hanging on her wall? To the right and left of the unrealistically thin and unblemished model are more catchy subtitles of articles within the magazine. On the very bottom of the cover of *Sugar* in alternating hot pink and yellow ink are the names of a few of the girl's favorite celebrities. She probably does not even open the magazine to probe further. She is off to find her parents to persuade them to buy the magazine. What messages are parents sending when they allow girls to read such material? What effect will it have on their daughters?

Without a doubt, *Sugar* and other "teen magazines" are published for an audience of pre-teen and teenage girls. The cover of the magazine does indeed serve its purposes by zoning in on what girls are discussing throughout school hallways every day. The editors know what appeals to young girls and how to exploit it. Thus, they have, for instance, the power to turn a passing interest in boys into an obsession. Simply by mentioning the word "boys" somewhere on the cover each month, they ensure sales to repeat customers. Are parents even aware of the flagrant disregard of the true consumer (parents) by the editors of teen magazines? For example, the editors have placed the following headline on the very cover of *Sugar*, "'Here's my credit card' and other things you wish your parents would say." Unfortunately, white lettering against a light blue background is easy to miss, and parents probably never even notice it on the cover of the magazine. Therefore, they are not encouraged to look further into the pages of the magazine. Obviously, family values and respect for authority figures are not ideas that interest the writers of the articles within this magazine.

However, even if parents are missing the boat on that point, there are other reasons to discourage young girls from reading teen magazines. The impossible-to-achieve physical images that girls try so hard to emulate are everywhere in *Sugar*. We know that when young girls find that they cannot be model-perfect, they are often devastated, and their self-esteem suffers. However, more than thirty-three percent—the majority—of the advertisements in *Sugar* focus on beauty products. All seem to portray the idea that girls will become beautiful, popular boy-magnets by using these products. The advertisers do not seem to care that a good portion of their audience might not even be allowed to wear make-up. All of the ads use typically attractive males and females in the forefront to catch the eye and hold the attention of the reader long enough for these ideas to penetrate. How do parents react to these magazines' messages? Do they give in and buy that tube of lipstick while reassuring young daughters that beauty is from within? However parents respond, clearly the influence on young girls by these magazines is, at times, overwhelming and overpowering.

While there are many negative and indeed false images throughout the pages of *Sugar*, it would appear that the magazine does give its reader the content promised by its cover. Of forty columns and articles, thirty percent either feature or significantly focus on boys. Celebrity highlights are only slightly less than the features on boys. Naturally, on the cover of the magazine, no reference was made to any articles discussing current events or informative topics. In fact, only one article in the entire magazine was truly informative and based on a topic about which young people might actually need to learn.

Finally, all of the images within *Sugar* magazine work together to put ideas into the impressionable minds of young girls. Every picture of a female shows a tall, slender, and flawless image that many young girls attempt to imitate. It is no wonder that suicide, eating disorders, and self-esteem problems are so prevalent among young people, especially young women. All of the images shown of males in the magazine are equally unrealistic. How will a woman ever be satisfied in a relationship if she is constantly seeking an image of perfection that does not exist? Yet what are parents doing to discourage these false images and encourage their daughters? How is it that images such as these are even being published? In truth, editors of teen magazines need to make a living just like everyone else. They know what interests young girls and how to exploit these interests to sell magazines. Publishers are aware that kids do not care about educational articles, and they know that many parents will buy the magazine for their children without scrutinizing the content of it. Certainly, these trends can be reversed simply by parents taking a more active, assertive role in what their children are reading. Parents must ensure that their children—in this case, especially young women—are educated about what is truly important: not image, but character.

Works Cited

Sugar, Britain's Best Selling Girls' Magazine. Oct. 2000.

The Masquerade of Patriotism

Sarah Breazeale

Assignment: In this out-of-class essay, the student was to respond to Norman Mailer's commentary Why Are We at War? *in a three page, formal essay.*

The catastrophic events of 9/11 led many people to re-evaluate their lives. The days and months following September 11, 2001 were filled with Americans flags, bumper stickers, and t-shirts. The flag was attached to almost anything. At times, the overzealous love that Americans suddenly had for their country was too much to bear—as if patriotism did not exist before 9/11. The flags were a reaction, for before 9/11, we did not think that our nation was great, we knew that it was. Afterwards, the expectations of Americans for their country were compromised, and Americans had constantly to re-affirm their status as a great nation. Even now, some are still overly patriotic.

The events of 9/11 were like having the rug pulled from underneath us. We were suddenly vulnerable. For so long we Americans had taken our freedom for granted, and the threat of others wanting to take that away left many feeling a renewed love for their nation, and a need to defend it. Flags were everywhere; proclamations of "these colors don't run!" were made, and acts of racial violence against Middle Easterners headlined on the national news. Americans waved their flags, suddenly bursting with pride for their nation and wanted the world to know that even a terrorist attack like 9/11 would not slow the United States down. Nevertheless, why did it take so many people dying to give Americans a wake-up call? We were, and still are, arrogant and have assumed that the United States was impenetrable. The resulting shock left us in a frenzy.

I thought that an attack on the United States was impossible. That belief changed on September 11, 2001 when my mother took my sister and me out of school and told us that buildings in New York had been hit by airplanes, and that my father was on lockdown at Warner Robins Air Force Base. While going to the orthodontist's office, footage of the Twin Towers in ruins was flashed on television and was the subject of every conversation in the building. For the first time, the idea of terrorism became real. I admit, I wore a pin of the American flag and had painted a small banner that said, "These colors don't fade!" Of course, I was in 8th grade and saw everyone else doing it, so it seemed like the right thing to do at the time. My then-13 year old self felt as if I had not appreciated my country before, and 9/11 made me realize that my country is a great nation, and I should love it for what it is. However, over time, that patriotism faded.

Citizens should be critical of their nation, for it helps to improve it. Norman Mailer makes an example in his book *Why Are We At War?* He writes, "The British have a love of their country that is profound. They can revile it, tell dirty stories about it, give you dish on all the imperfects who are running the country. But their patriotism is deep" (Mailer 15). In contrast, many Americans assume that the United States is the greatest nation in the world; therefore, there is no room for ridicule. They have not seen an exact image, but more of an ideal that they have held America up to, and in the end, the ideal does not hold up.

Immediately after the attacks, many Americans had a false sense of patriotism. At first, they went with the flow, and did what everyone else was doing. Their feelings were not real, or had only a bit of truth at their roots. But months passed, and that so-called patriotism started to ebb away, until they felt the same way as they did before 9/11. For some, their pride in the U.S. was real, but for many it was just something they felt they had to display. Americans felt insecure about their country after 9/11, after so much death and sorrow, that doing anything but expressing pride seemed to be a sign of weakness.

While 9/11 was tragic, and did open many people's eyes to the harsh reality of the world, many Americans set themselves up to be vulnerable because of their arrogance concerning the United States. In the end, they set themselves up for a shock when 9/11 occurred. One has to wonder, though, if there were to be another attack on American soil, would we react the same way again? Would flags fly high, or has 9/11 taught many Americans an important lesson? I would like to think that we learned something from 9/11, but I fear that the American ego would emerge once more.

Works Cited

Mailer, Norman. *Why Are We At War?* New York: Random House Trade Paperbacks, 2003.

Spanking: An Acceptable Form of Discipline

Janice Fisher

Assignment: In this out-of-class assignment, the student was to develop an argumentative essay based on a topic from an approved list.

While there is a significant difference between child abuse and a mere disciplinary spanking, in today's society, one might be coerced into believing that they are one and the same. Many advocates of eliminating spanking have become vocal in their intent to make it a crime for a parent to spank a child under any circumstances, for any reason. Using the words "child abuse" to get the attention of Americans, these advocates will argue that a person who uses any form of spanking falls under the definition of a child abuser. This is wrong because it confuses those who use spanking as a form of discipline with people who hit children for pleasure or emotional release. In order for discipline to be effective, it must be administered in a controlled manner, unlike that of a child abuser who will strike a child in an uncontrolled fit of anger. Most family counseling professionals would agree with Dr. Dobson's statement: "I can only tell you that there is not a single well-designed scientific study that confirms the hypothesis that spanking by a loving parent breeds violence in children" (138). Although it is unfortunate that child abuse is so prevalent in the United States, it should not be associated with loving parents who choose to use spanking as a form of discipline.

A primary argument of anti-spanking advocates is that a child who is spanked will become a violent person because of the physical punishment inflicted upon him. John Rosemond, in his column "Good Parenting," states, "There is no good scientifically grounded evidence that would suggest spankings per se incline children toward violent behavior" (2 D). As a child, I was occasionally disciplined with "the belt." If we disobeyed my father, a possible consequence was that he would spank us. Neither my siblings nor I have grown up to be "hitters." We understood that the spanking was a consequence of our wrongdoing. It is the responsibility of the parents to decide what their family disciplinary policy will be and to ensure that their children understand this policy.

The use of "the belt" was not the only discipline method my parents used, as the punishment should be compatible with the circumstance of the infraction. In the article, "When to Spank," Lynn Rossellini suggests, "The best disciplinary approach is to use a number of methods including . . . timeouts, rewards, withdrawal of privileges . . ." because "spanking seems to work in conjunction with some of these techniques" (5). Depending on the personality of the child and the type and frequency of the offense, the parent must decide what type of discipline is best-suited to bring about correction. It may be effective to put a child in "timeout" or to subject the child to a loss of privileges, thus avoiding a spanking. However, at times, a spanking may be the best way to curtail the unacceptable behavior. It is also important for a parent to be consistent in discipline simply because a child needs to know his boundaries and the consequences of crossing them.

When a spanking is chosen as an appropriate form of discipline, it must be administered in a manner that will not injure the child. Professionals agree that the proper part of the body to spank is the buttocks area, "where permanent damage is very unlikely" (Dobson 142). It is also the general consensus to apply the spanking with an open hand. I do not agree with that and prefer the use of a paddle to administer a spanking. If I have the paddle in my hands, my children recognize the reason for it and expect a spanking. I do not want my children to feel threatened by my hands. Typically, children will exhibit their worst behavior when they are in public, which usually incites the parent to anger, making it awkward to discipline. When faced with public outbursts, the use of verbal correction is best. A minor outburst could possibly be ignored. When a child sees that he is not getting any attention for his behavior, he will most likely stop. Another tactic to use is to distract the child from the cause of his ill temper, allowing time for both the child and parent to calm down, therefore eliminating the need for discipline. It is essential to remember the ultimate goal of spanking: "You're not trying to cause pain; you're simply relaying the message that the behavior was unacceptable" (Kashani 83).

In addition to being administered appropriately, a spanking should be used only on children who are old enough to understand what their parents' standard of behavior is and the consequences of rebelling against that standard. Most toddlers can comprehend right from wrong and can be dissuaded with light spanking or a tap on the hand. On the other hand, an older child may be more affected by a loss of privileges for unacceptable behavior than by physical punishment. For example, when a toddler disobeys his parents' directive, such as to pick up his toys, he probably will have a different attitude if he receives a spanking after refusing to obey the first time. However, an eight-year-old who does not pick up his toys may be more apt to obey if he understands that the consequence of his refusal is to lose the privilege of watching his favorite television program. Using common sense is required when choosing the right type of discipline that will bring about a change in the child's behavior.

Parents are responsible for training their children to become independent adults; within this responsibility lies the task of disciplining. The decision of how discipline is handled must belong to the parent. Although advocates against spanking will argue that, in every instance, it is abuse, a properly-administered spanking by a loving parent is an acceptable form of discipline. According to John Rosemond, family psychologist, "When a child who is secure in his parents' love is spanked by those parents, he does not consider himself the victim of a violent act" (2 D). It is imperative that parents maintain the right to choose spanking as a form of discipline, as deemed necessary.

Works Cited

Dobson, James. *Solid Answers*. Wheaton: Tyndale, 1997.

Kashani, Javid H., et al. *Raising Happy Children: A Parent's Guide*. New York: Three Rivers, 1998.

Rosemond, John. "There's No Proof Spanking IS Hurtful: Good Parenting." *Macon Telegraph* 20 April 1999: 2D.

Rossellini, Lynn. "When to Spank." *US News & World Report*. 124. 14 April 1998: 52–58. GALILEO.

The Struggle of Women in Uniform

Shanan Denise Rivera

Assignment: In this out-of-class assignment, the student was to develop an argumentative essay using two or more online sources.

Women who have the courage to put on a uniform every day to defend our country face many barriers. Like men, women must deploy to locations around the world. And, like men, women go into war-torn countries not knowing if they will see tomorrow. Given the similarities, why are women treated differently than men in the military? There should not be any form of discrimination in the military, particularly on the basis of gender. Women in the military are trained in the same manner as their male counterparts. Military women deserve equal and just treatment comparable to military men. Merit, not gender, should be the deciding factor for reprimand or recognition of any military members.

Since its beginning, the military has withheld positions from women based merely on gender. Prior to World War II, women were not permitted in combat positions. History was changed with the induction of the Women's Air Force Service Pilots (WASPS) into military service. These women flew military aircraft built in U.S. factories across the Atlantic Ocean to Great Britain for the war effort. Some were shot down and killed during these vital missions. Former WASP Karen Godfrey exclaims, "It was the sacrifice and bravery of women in uniform that made the victory in World War II and afterwards possible" (Masko, "Women" 1). Throughout military history, the role of women has been diminished. Only now, after fifty years, has recognition finally been given for the efforts of the WASPS. These women, during World War II, courageously gave their lives and inadvertently set the pathway for future women. The struggle has been great, but the fight is not yet over. Secretary of the Air Force Shelia Widnall states, "As the Air Force realizes that performance, not gender, is what counts when you put together an all volunteer force, more and more positions open up to women" (Widnall 2). Men have finally relinquished their fighter cockpits to women, but male attitudes, for the most part, have remained unchanged since women were first allowed to wear the uniform.

The negative attitude of some military men interferes with women's progress and with the mission. Based on my seven-year military career as an Aircraft Structural Maintenance Specialist and as the only woman in a twenty-man shop, my conclusion is that men range from tolerant to defiant when they consider women in the military. Like most women in maintenance career fields, I had to work twice as hard as my male counterparts to earn respect. The men in my shop thought I fell into the stereotype of a woman trying to do a man's job. Secretary of the Air Force Shelia Widnall says, ". . . the role of military women is to serve their country in whatever capacity they can, without artificial barriers based solely on gender" (1). For example, a male recruit, who arrived a month after me, was upgraded six months before me. Although the quality of my work was far superior, I was not given the chance to succeed. While the new recruit was working on the aircraft and receiving training, I was scraping paint off the shop floor. I was brushed aside while he excelled. Denying me training almost impeded the unit's mission. When aircraft returned from the Gulf War needing rapid maintenance, everyone needed to be utilized. Former Defense Secretary Dick Cheney agrees by saying, ". . . we couldn't have won the [Gulf] war without women" (qtd. in Widnall 1). With the limited amount of knowledge acquired, I was presented an opportunity to demonstrate my ability. To everyone's surprise, I surpassed all expectations. The unsatisfactory treatment I received was incentive to work harder and better than any of the men in that shop. Once I showed the quality of my work and dedication to my job, attitudes began to change.

The attitudes of men have shifted tremendously over the years once women were given an opportunity to progress in their military careers. Even through my terrible work experiences with men, nothing stopped me from being the best worker I could be. At first, some men were hostile because they shared the thoughts of my fellow co-workers. Others were flirtatious, expecting more than just a job well done. After two years of working harder than I ever had in my entire life, I began to reap respect and rewards. I was being asked for by name to work on the aircraft by the men who previously showed animosity toward me. Brigadier General Chuck Yeager says it best: "From a pilot's standpoint, it really doesn't make that much difference in our Air Force. Gal or guy, they're really, really good" (Masko, "NATO" 2). I always felt my work was a reflection of me; therefore, I completed my job proficiently and professionally every time. Over the years, I have received numerous letters of recognition and fourteen medals, seven for outstanding achievement. At the end of my career, I had finally achieved my goal. Men were not perceiving me as just a woman, but as a professional who would accomplish every necessary task promptly and efficiently to achieve mission effectiveness.

Although more steps are taken now to generate opportunities for women, the struggle is not over, and women are continually discriminated against in the military. I trust that my seven-year battle to disprove stereotypes opened or at least cracked a few doors for women wanting to join the military. I agree with Major General Marcelite J. Harris, the first African-American two-star woman general in the U.S. Armed Forces, who said, "In order to maintain readiness and effectiveness, the United States will need to draw more and more from the talent pool of women who want careers in the military" (Masko, "NATO" 1). Men no longer dominate the military. To remain the best military force in the world, supervisors must recognize the abilities of the individual and look past gender. Denying qualified women positions in the military is denying our country its most effective and efficient line of defense.

Works Cited

Masko, David P. "The Women Who Built the Air Force." 11 Nov. 1997. <http://www.afmil/news/Nov1996/nl996 1108961130.html>.

Masko, David P. "NATO Women Discuss Their Vital Role in Military's Success." 11 Nov. 1997. <http://www.afmil/news/June 1996/ nl996062196599.html>.

Widnall, Shelia, E. "From WAFs to Warriors: A Reflection of Women in the United States Air Force." 11 Nov. 1997. <http://www.afmil/ news/speech/current/From WAFs to Warriors A R.html>.

A Crack in the Rainbow

Joel Bartholf

Assignment: In this out-of-class assignment, the student was to choose a controversial topic and develop an argument in support of a specific position.

Flying low into the target zone under the sweeping radar of the air-security watch, the aerial assault team makes final preparations for a jump into the dark canopy of the nighttime skies. Meanwhile, the ground troops scale the perimeter fence and advance slowly, using the cover of shadows to avoid detection by surveillance equipment. This scene may appear to have been taken from a block-buster movie, but actually it has become much too frequently associated with the tactics used by eco-warriors from the environmental activist group known as Greenpeace. Ironically, the controversial strategies that once brought Greenpeace both recognition and international appeal have recently caused internal conflicts and a loss of public support. Should Greenpeace rely on eco-warrior tactics and headline grabbing stunts, or should it pursue a more subtle and perhaps more effective strategy of environmental diplomacy?

In 1971, a small crew of determined protesters sailed through the icy cold waters of the north Pacific Ocean ("Greenpeace" 2). Driven by the concept that they could make a difference, the crew piloted a tiny fishing boat from Vancouver to the coast of Alaska; their purpose was to protest the atmospheric nuclear testing being conducted by the United States on the island of Amchitka. This island off the coast of Alaska was home to several species of endangered wildlife, including the peregrin falcon, the bald eagle, and various types of marine mammals. The island was also situated on an area that was known to have more seismic activity than any other place on earth, thus raising even greater concerns of unforeseeable dangers. Even though the nuclear tests were not halted until 1972, this journey gave birth to the group that would become the largest environmental organization in the world, Greenpeace ("Greenpeace" 2–3).

Today Greenpeace is a multilevel corporation consisting of nearly 3 million members worldwide and an annual budget of $140 million dollars. It has 12 offices located in the United States and a total of 43 offices spanning the globe; these offices are manned by a full-time staff of 1,000 employees (Toufexis 1). The purpose of the organization as described by Greenpeace is to "create a green and peaceful world by drawing attention to an abuse of the environment through the unwavering presence at the scene, whatever the risk." Greenpeace goes on to state that it "embraces the principle of non-violence, rejecting attacks on people and property." By the use of "creative confrontation," the organization pledges to "force solutions to global environmental problem" ("Greenpeace" 1–2).

In recent years, Greenpeace's image and credibility have suffered repeated blows. The passion that many of its members have for their cause has been manifested in excessive acts of aggression. Although the organization publicly denounces the use of violence or attacks on people and property, this claim often seems to be a decoy for the truth. The historical files located on the Greenpeace International web page can attest to this claim. The files are loaded with different articles showing how the organization takes matters into its own hands in the name of environmental justice. In many instances in the past, so that it could dodge the responsibility, Greenpeace has been able to use the excuse that the incidents were carried out by groups of activists acting on their own accord. This concept was used in a case involving a Norwegian fishing vessel rammed by activists, but the court was not fooled by the decoy and held Greenpeace liable for the damages (Steele 1).

During July of 1995, Greenpeace activists forcefully occupied an aging oil storage platform named Brent Spar. The platform was scheduled to be towed out to the deep waters of the Atlantic where it would then be sunk. The activists, who insisted the rig must be disposed of on land, claimed that they had saved the ocean from pollution by some 5,000 tons of crude oil mixed with radioactive sludge. They were later forced to admit the potential ecological damage had been gravely miscalculated. The oil platform contained less than 10 tons of residue, and most scientists actually supported the idea of disposal at sea. During the 23-day occupation, Shell gasoline stations across the world were picketed by protesters and activists. In Frankfurt, Germany, gun shots blasted through one Shell station, while in Hamburg yet another station was firebombed ("Brent" 1–2). The false allegations, getting out of hand, cost the Shell company more than 2 million dollars, not including the damages caused by the international boycott of their stations (Brunet 3).

Greenpeace co-founder and environmental activist Dr. Patrick Moore warns that "there has been an increase in radical environmentalism in the 1990's and that itself poses a significant threat to the environment" (Brunet 2). Dr. Moore was involved in the creation of Greenpeace in 1971 and was chairman from 1977 to 1979 (Brunet 2). He became increasingly dissatisfied with the organization in the mid 1980's and finally left of his own volition in 1986 ("Warning" 1). Although he remains proud of his accomplishments and active in the environmental arena, he no longer supports Greenpeace because he feels that it has become a form of "eco-extremism." He states that "their instinct is to go for the jugular at every opportunity, back-stab and lie, and eventually there will be nobody left who trusts them" (Brunet 2).

Without the shared view of the public, Greenpeace would cease to exist because it relies primarily on private donations. The virtue of accuracy is imperative if Greenpeace expects to remain credible in the eyes of its supporters. A sharp drop in memberships and monetary contributions recently might suggest that the organization has begun to lose some of its credibility and shared vision. The loss of available money has forced the organization to make cutbacks in full-time personnel and branch locations. Although several branches have remained strong, such as those located in Germany, other branches, including the U.S. chapters, have experienced dismal contributions (Steele 1–2). This year more than one regional office fell victim to cutbacks because of budget concerns. The regional branch in Atlanta, Georgia, was among the offices closed.

The dismal performance of offices located in the United States and other branches abroad has raised concerns and sparked conflicts within Greenpeace. Its members have become divided over the issues facing the future of the organization and what position it should take. Some members feel that in the future, there should be a shift from the primarily frontline activism towards a more politically active approach by bringing the environmental issues to where the decisions are made. They believe that the time is right for a more practical solution to the environmental issues facing the planet. Many other members within Greenpeace, on the other hand, strongly oppose any reduction of confrontation. They insist that the organization needs to place more activists, not fewer, on the front-line (Toufexis 2).

I am very sympathetic to some of Greenpeace's causes. Yet in good conscience, I cannot support the organization nor condone its actions. The issues facing the environment must be dealt with because they can no longer be pushed aside. As human beings, we have abused our planet for entirely too long and will all ultimately suffer the consequences if measures are not taken to amend our current situation. However, the use of forceful and extreme tactics inevitably compels the recipients to assume a defensive position in order to protect themselves from the aggressive onslaught. Positive change is most often a product of time, planning, and most importantly cooperation. In order for environmental issues to be resolved, the offenders and environmental specialists must work together instead of constantly opposing one another.

Greenpeace must reform its current use of "extreme" tactics in order to salvage its public image. Each time the research it conducts is incorrect or a protest gets out of control, the ramifications come back to haunt the organization, and the credibility gap widens. The up-front confrontation must give way to cooperation and practical solutions. If significant changes are not made soon, Greenpeace, not the forests and species that it tries to protect, will become extinct.

Works Cited

"Brent Spar: The Environment: Book of the Year (1996)." *Encyclopedia Britannica Online*. Online. GALILEO. 28 Nov. 1997.

Brunet, Robin. "The Spirit of Sanity." *Alberta Report/Wester Report* 11 Dec. 1995. *Academic Abstracts Full Text*. CD-ROM. Ebsco. Nov. 1997.

"Greenpeace International Homepage." 28 Oct. 1997. <http://www.greenpeace.html>.

Steele, Scott. "Rainbow Warriors." *Maclean's* 09 Sept. 1996. *Academic Abstracts Full Test.* CD-ROM. Ebsco. Nov. 1997.

Toufexis, Anastasia. "It's Not Easy Being Greenpeace." *Time* 16 Nov. 1995. *Academic Abstracts Full Text.* CD-ROM. Ebsco. Nov. 1997.

"Warning From An Ex-Greenpeace Leader." 28 Oct. 1997. Available <http://www.gpeacex.html>.

Pop's Tradition

Miriam Hosey

Assignment: In this in-class final exam essay, the student was to write a narration about a meaningful family tradition.

When John McPeak embarked on *Columbia*, the ship that brought him to his new American home in the early part of the twentieth century, he took with him many of the values and traditions that his family held dear. As my grandfather grew into his role as an American, without realizing it, he started some new traditions. These rituals are still carried out each year in the homes of his grandchildren.

Pop's favorite American assimilation was his passion for the game of baseball. My grandfather discovered baseball and fell in love with it. He saw his team, the Phillies, through good seasons and bad ones. He watched star hitters come and go. With his loyalty never wavering, Pop gave each new player, from young rookies like Ritchie Asburn to noted veterans like Jim Bunning and Steve Carlton, a fair chance. He even enjoyed a few good pennant races. Pop rejoiced as the Whiz Kids claimed the National League title in 1950 and nursed their egos in 1964 when the St. Louis Cardinals dashed their hopes of victory. All of this occurred under the observant eyes of his seven children and twenty-one grandchildren.

With each new spring season, like clockwork, we watched Pop become a kid again. He would eagerly await news of his favorite team's performance. I can remember Pop flipping through the sports section of the Philadelphia *Enquirer* to get a report on his beloved Phillies. Throwing down the paper, he would fill the room with his Irish brogue. His rant would always be, "Ah, what a bunch of bums! Sissies, the whole lot of them!"

Summer days would pass into nights, and Pop could always be found in his favorite spot sitting on the patio with a lit pipe in one hand and his transistor radio in the other. Through the crackling and static, he would listen intently as the Phils beat up on the Reds, or vice versa. If he would invite one of us to join him, a lesson would begin. Pete Rose, Mike Schmidt, Larry Bowa, etc., the roster would run through a child's head until he or she had it memorized. The youngster never realized that he or she was learning while Pop never realized he was teaching.

In late August, 1976, after a heated debate over the Phillies' poor performance, Pop went to bed and suffered a massive stroke. He would die a few weeks later. The Phillies never pulled out of their slump that year. Things turned around for the team by 1980 when they won the World Series. Cousins called from Phoenix to celebrate. I am sure that Pop celebrated too. When Mike Schmidt told all of the fans to savor the moment, I am sure Pop would have agreed with the star infielder.

Although many years have passed since Pop sat on the patio with his transistor radio, his baseball tradition continues still. On Father's Day, 2002, my family headed out to Veteran's Stadium in Philadelphia. This time little one-year-old Ricky joined the clan. He came home with a certificate to document the occasion. Without knowing it, Ricky was continuing in a tradition started by his great-grandfather when he first heard the whack of a ball in the same city, almost a century ago.

Small Towns Still Hold Big Promises

Gail Odom

Assignment: In this in-class final exam essay, the student was to compare or contrast the depiction of small towns in current movies or television shows with those that Benjamin Stein discusses in his essay "Whatever Happened to Small-town America?"

In Benjamin Stein's essay "Whatever Happened to Small Town America?" he discussed how cultural attitudes toward small towns have changed over the years. They have indeed changed, although not necessarily for the worse. While Hollywood writers and film-makers do often portray small towns as ". . . places where bad things happen to innocent people," as Stein suggests, these towns are also places where people are friendly and trustworthy and where the family is of great importance. I think Hollywood depicts this positive view as well, albeit with more subtlety, as seen in such movies as *Doc Hollywood* and *Sleeping With the Enemy*.

Much like Stein's description of Jim Rockford damaging his car and suffering financial and physical grief at the hands of a town bloated by corruption, Michael J. Fox suffers a similar fate as Ben, the character he portrays in the film *Doc Hollywood*. Ben is a sur-geon en route to a prestigious new job as Chief of Staff at a hospi-tal in Los Angeles. Traveling down a country road through a small town in South Carolina, Ben swerves his car to avoid a herd of cattle crossing the road, and plunges his car, a brand new Porsche, into a nearby fence. Rather than receiving the apology he expects from the owner of the cattle (and consequently, the fence), he gets yelled at by the owner for damaging his fence. Before he can speak, the sheriff of the town arrives and gives the doctor a citation for reckless driving. Of course, Ben has no cash to pay the fine, only credit cards and personal checks; and the court, over which the sheriff presides as judge, cannot accept out-of-town checks. Therefore, "Doc" is sentenced to serving forty-eight hours of community service as physician at the local hospital. Conveniently, the resident physician there is out sick and he's the only doctor in town. However, in spite of the fact that they acquire his services deceitfully and illegally, you almost can't blame these people because they only did these things to help the sick in their town, and who can find fault with that?

The town begins to grow on Ben. He likes the familiarity of the people, the time they take to stop and speak to one another on the street. He's been used to the fast pace of city life, and when he stops and takes a moment to look around, he sees things in a different light. He even meets a woman from the town and falls in love. In fact, when it's finally time for him to escape from his "prison" and continue his journey to California and his posh, new private practice, he trades in his business suit for a pair of blue jeans, and he ends up staying in the small town after all.

Sleeping With the Enemy supports Stein's belief that small towns appear on screen as places where evil lurks behind every corner. Just like the film *Bad Day at Black Rock* that Stein mentions, a murder takes place in a small, quiet town. Julia Roberts' character Laura tries to escape a life of physical and mental abuse from her husband by fleeing to a small town in Idaho. Although her husband, a deranged psychopath, does track her down and there is a frightful and violent confrontation that ends with Laura shooting and killing her husband, positive small-town qualities and characteristics are still visibly noticeable throughout the film. For instance, Laura picks apples from her front yard and makes homemade apple pie, an American small-town tradition. She leaves the kitchen door open at night. She is also befriended by a man who lives next door to her, and he teaches her to trust again and eventually to love again.

In big cities, people barely glance at one another in passing, much less take the time to befriend a neighbor. Most people don't even know who their neighbors are. How many people in big cities would feel safe enough to leave their doors open without fear of burglary or an attack of some sort? I would imagine that there are very few, if any. Surely, one might find evil, danger, and corruption in a small town, but no place is completely free of all those things. They exist everywhere to some degree. However, in a smaller town, the rate and/or frequency of such situations or occurrences are to a much lesser degree than in a big city. When Hollywood films show the vicious side of small towns, I think they do so not to prey upon or ridicule these places, but to show that they are not free from these criminal acts either. It portrays them a little more realistically without denying the charm these towns possess as well. Overall, small towns still hold that special appeal that has attracted so many people for so long.

Pressures of Society in "Battle Royal" and "The Lottery"

Dorothy Tetzlaff-Taylor

Assignment: In this out-of-class essay, the student was to develop a paper in which he or she considers the impact of a person's family, church, culture, history, and traditions on his or her development.

Many times we do something to go along with the crowd, even when we know it is the wrong thing to do. Picking on another child because of his freckles, drinking underage at a high school party, or gossiping about a co-worker—we've all been guilty of this "pack mentality" at one time or another. The question is: why do we do this? We do it because it is easier than standing up for what we know is right, because we want to be accepted by our peers, and because we are afraid of the personal consequences if we try to change a situation and we fail. This is also true for many of the characters in the short stories "Battle Royal" and "The Lottery." This social pressure to fit in motivates them to participate in and accept practices that are morally reprehensible.

In "Battle Royal," Ralph Ellison describes in rich detail the circumstances surrounding a smoker and battle royal. Smokers were a common occurrence in the early part of the 20th century, particularly across the southern Unite States, and involved wealthy men gathering to eat, drink, and smoke cigars. The battle royal, which served as part of the evening's entertainment, entailed blindfolding a group of young men and watching them fight it out in a boxing ring until only two contenders were left. Those two would then compete for a monetary prize. It sounds innocent enough, right? Now, if one considers the fact that the wealthy men were all white and the young fighters were all black, it becomes obvious that this ritual is about much more than just an entertaining night out with the guys. The whites use it as a tool to keep blacks in an inferior position in society by belittling, humiliating, and frightening them. One of the men spells this out for the narrator when he says, "We mean to do right by you, but you've got to know your place at all times" (159).

The men who instigate the ritual are "some of the most impor-tant men of the town . . . bankers, lawyers, judges, doctors, fire chiefs, teachers, merchants. Even one of the more fashionable pastors" (151). They presumably enjoy their position within the community and intend to keep things the way they are. Ellison introduces evidence of their greed and gluttony with descriptive imagery like "wolfing down the buffet foods" (152) and "hungrily, his lips loose and drooling" (152). There is also a level of cowardice implied by the fact that the men hold this ritual "in the main ballroom of the leading hotel," on their own turf, ensuring that the black boys will be uncomfortable with their surroundings, easier to control, and less likely to protest when things start to get out of hand (151). I would argue that even some of these powerful, white men may be influenced by peer pressure to be there, and are not as malicious individually as they are as a group. Although they go along with most of the night's events, when things begin to get too chaotic and a few of the drunker men start to toss the stripper about the room, "[s]ome of the more sober ones [help] her to escape" (153). And when the narrator is giving his speech, most of "the men were still talking and laughing . . . but a few of [them], especially the superintendent, were listening" (158). I believe that this is evidence that they do not necessarily agree with everything that is happen-ing in the ballroom, but do not know how to blatantly object without being ostracized by the rest of the group.

The young black men, who are the victims, seem a bit naïve. The narrator idealistically thinks that the affluent white men have invited him to the smoker out of respect for him and a desire to hear his graduation speech. He agrees to take part in the battle royal mostly because of his desperation to impress them and be accepted into their world. The other boys, classmates of the narrator, seem to be there for the money. They have each been promised five dollars for their participation, and they are annoyed that the narrator, "by taking part in the fight, had knocked one of their friends out of a night's work" (151). It is unclear as to whether or not they know what the evening has in store for them and just accept it, or if the experience is as confusing to them as it is to the narrator. Even though they have been "hired" for the event, it becomes clear that the boys are not free to leave if they choose to when the narrator tells us that one of them "began to plead to go home" (152) and again when "the men began to push [them] onto the [electrified] rug" (157) keeping them engaged in the activity against their will. Fear of even harsher consequences keeps them from fighting back.

By night's end, the narrator still does not seem to fully understand the purpose of the evening. He is overjoyed by the gifts bestowed upon him by the important men in town. He is blind to the fact that, even though they have given him a college scholarship, the men are only rewarding his obedience and acceptance that he is of an inferior race. They never intend for him to be anything other than a lesser member of society, and surely never on an equal level with themselves. They are counting on the fact that he will help maintain this social hierarchy by "lead[ing] his people in the proper paths" (159), by teaching them that blacks need to be aware of their subordinate place in society, to follow the rules imposed upon them by whites, and to be grateful for the few opportunities that they do have.

In "The Lottery," Shirley Jackson illustrates for us an even more barbaric practice. Once a year, the villagers in her story gather together and randomly select a person to be stoned to death. This annual event serves two purposes. Initially, begun generations earlier as an annual sacrifice to a god or goddess of the harvest, it served to ensure a fruitful season. This idea has been maintained and passed down with the expression, 'Lottery in June, corn be heavy soon' (247). I contend, however, that a deeper reason for the continuation of the ritual has evolved over time. I think it enforces the strong work ethic that is valued in the community. Jackson establishes this pressure to be perceived as productive when Mr. Summers says, "guess we better get started . . . so's we can go back to work," and when Tessie Hutchinson arrives late, she excuses herself by saying, "[w]ouldn't have me leave m'dishes in the sink, now would you, Joe?" (245). The characters may believe, if only on a subconscious level, that living their life in a virtuous way through honest, hard work will spare them from the fate of the lottery. Old Man Warner demonstrates this as he brags that this is his "[s]eventy-seventh year . . . in the lottery," yet he has still not been selected (247).

Unlike Ellison's "Battle Royal," the characters in Jackson's story are not as easy to define as good or bad, victim or predator. There is no clear antagonist, and it appears, on the surface at least, that all of the members of the community have an equal chance of being chosen. Although the events unfold on common ground in the town square, there is still a hint of social hierarchy in the village. The lottery is conducted by Mr. Summers, who owns a coal company, and Mr. Graves, the postmaster, with the assistance of Mr. Martin, the village grocer, and his son. When the people start to gather, the rest of the men discuss "planting and rain, tractors and taxes," indicating that the remainder of the community is primarily made up of farming families (244). We could draw from this that there is a disparity between the business class and working class in the community and the power they each hold.

The tradition of the annual lottery is slowly being worn down as "much of the ritual [has] been forgotten or discarded" (244) or has "changed with time" (245). There are a few, mainly the women of the village, who show evidence of resistance to its continuation. Tessie Hutchinson shows her disrespect for the event by forgetting what day it is and arriving late, and Mrs. Delacroix exhibits her veiled defiance when she states that it "[s]eems like there's no time at all between the lotteries anymore . . . Seems like we got through with the last one only last week" (246). Some are a little more obvious, like Mr. and Mrs. Adams who mention that some villages are "talking of giving up the lottery" and other "places have already quit lotteries" (247). When they do this, they are met with hostility and ridicule by Old Man Warner as he says to them, "[p]ack of crazy fools . . . Next thing you know, they'll be wanting to go back to living in caves, nobody work any more . . . There's *always* been a lottery" (247). Warner's comment about work reinforces the theory that maintaining a strong work ethic in the community has become the main purpose of the ritual.

Despite the mild resistance of a few characters, the custom continues because none of them have the courage to openly protest it for fear of how the others will react. They may even believe that their rebelliousness will be seen as a resistance of the work ethic, increasing their chances of becoming the victim of the next session of the lottery. Evidently, the children share this idea as "the feeling of liberty [sits] uneasily on most of them" (243). School is out for the summer, yet they continue to talk about "the classroom and teacher, of books and reprimands" and intuitively seek out work, like gathering the stones, to keep themselves busy and productive (243). This demonstrates their submission to the pressure to honor the tradition of the lottery, which is surely learned from their parents. The practice will be carried on through the children's involvement, which includes even the youngest of them. Little Davy Hutchinson is so young that he does not understand the lottery, and even needs help drawing his slip of paper. But, when his mother is finally chosen and it is time to stone her, he is forced to participate when "someone [gives him] a few pebbles" to throw (249).

We are all susceptible to pressure from our peers, society as a whole, and from ourselves. The characters in our literature are no different. In "Battle Royal," the white men are influenced by their peers to humiliate and degrade the blacks to maintain the status quo, and the blacks are compelled by their fear to just accept the cruel treatment and not rock the boat. In Jackson's story, the characters are goaded into agreeing with the lottery, and ultimately committing murder, because of the pressure to appear hard working and virtuous. It is shocking what people can be persuaded to take part in, just out of a need to fit in, and both of these stories serve as a warning of what can happen if we allow ourselves to stray from our own values just for the sake of conformity.

Works Cited

Ellison, Ralph. "Battle Royal." *Literature and Its Writers: A Compact Introduction to Fiction, Poetry and Drama*, 3rd ed. Ed. Ann Charters and Samuel Charters. Boston: Bedford/St. Martin's, 2004. 150–160.

Jackson, Shirley. "The Lottery." *Literature and Its Writers: A Compact Introduction to Fiction, Poetry, and Drama*, 3rd ed. Ed. Ann Charters and Samuel Charters. Boston: Bedford/St. Martin's, 2004. 243–249.

The Influence of Childhood Experiences

Carolyn Whitt

Assignment: In this out-of-class essay, the student was to compare two short stories in terms of theme.

Most people can recall incidents from their childhood that have had a lasting effect upon them. Traumatic childhood experiences cannot be easily forgotten, nor their impressions erased from memory. Indeed, such memories, even when recalled years later, may elicit strong feelings of love or hate, influence a person's life, and even alter the course of one's future. William Faulkner's "Barn Burning" and Richard Russo's "The Whore's Child" show vastly different responses to disturbing childhood experiences and how such responses can positively or negatively impact one's future.

In Faulkner's "Barn Burning," Sarty Snopes is a young boy who suffers psychological and physical abuse at the hand of his father. Sarty's father Abner is a cold, hard man whose deceptive life revolves around his unbending pride in himself, and as a result the family suffers severe poverty. The family has had to move often as a result of Abner's habitual way of handling a grudge against another man by burning down the offender's barn. Sarty is deeply troubled by his father's defiance of truth and justice, and when Abner is taken to court under suspicion of barn burning, and Sarty is brought forward as a tentative witness, he glances at his father and thinks, "with frantic grief and despair, *He aims for me to lie, and I will have to do hit*"

(400). Sarty is torn between family loyalty and honesty. The judge seems to feel sorry for Sarty and does not force him to testify against his father. Abner senses his son's inner struggle, and later that day he harshly accuses Sarty: "You were fixing to tell them. You would have told him" (402). Sarty does not answer, so his father strikes him on the side of the head.

When the Snopes family arrives at a new place to work for the wealthy gentleman Major de Spain, Sarty dares to hope that there is a bit of integrity left in his father that will change him "from what maybe he can't help but be" (404). However, the bit of hope that Sarty has is soon crushed by the awful knowledge that Abner is again reverting to his former method of retaliation because his new employer has wounded his pride. In a sudden moment of inspiration, Sarty knows the time has come to heed to the integrity of his heart instead of the authority of this man whom he has tried in vain to respect and defend. Desperately "sobbing for breath" (410), he rushes to warn de Spain, knowing this gesture is the only thing within his power that can perhaps right this injustice. Sarty never stops running, but now his feet carry him away from the man he has called "Pap" (407), the man who has devastated his childhood. He runs frantically away from the only people he knows because he realizes that he can never be happy with the life they offer him. With tremendous courage, Sarty responds in a positive way to his traumatic experiences. He turns the course of his future from its downward trajectory to a life that will allow him moral integrity.

Sister Ursula, in Russo's "The Whore's Child," experiences a traumatic and tragic childhood as well, but unlike Sarty, she succumbs to this negative influence and never escapes its shadow. Ursula is the daughter of a prostitute to whom, of course, she is only a useless burden. As a young child, Ursula is taken to a convent by the man she adores and innocently believes is her father: "In the convent," Ursula recalls, "I was known as the whore's child" (506). Because of her background, the nuns show her no sympathy as the other children make her into "a suitable object for their crudest derision" (507).

Like Sarty, Ursula feels trapped in a world of confusion and despair. She holds on to the hope that her "father" will come rescue her, much as Sarty holds to the hope that his father will become a respectable man. Because the man Ursula believes to be her father is actually her mother's pimp, her hopes never materialize. Despite her longing to escape the misery of the convent, Ursula stays, thinking her father will be able to find her if she stays where he left her. Ursula, full of bitterness and hatred, resigns herself to spending her life with these "useless women" (512) and becomes Sister Ursula, "a hateful nun" (515). She does not realize the truth about the man she thinks is her father until she is an old woman. In looking back, she realizes how this deception ruined her life. She had not realized what kind of man her 'father' was and had spent her life in the shadow of his empty promise to return for her.

Sarty's and Sister Ursula's traumatic childhood experiences are the results of parents who are unconcerned about their children's future. Every child longs for parents who are worthy of their love and respect, but as in Sarty's and Sister Ursula's situations, when parents fail, it is left to the child to decide how to respond to the disappointment. A few may find the strength and courage to respond positively, as Sarty does, and let the disappointment motivate them to become people of integrity; however, all too often, such a traumatic childhood will produce a bitter, hateful person such as poor Ursula who does not see the reality of her situation until she is too old to change. It is difficult for a child to excel in life when he or she is forced to deal with disappointments like those faced by Sarty and Ursula. Every child needs a trustworthy person to guide his or her life in a positive direction.

Works Cited

Faulkner, William. "Barn Burning." *The Compact Bedford Introduction to Literature*. Ed. Michael Meyer. 7th ed. Boston: Bedford-St. Martin's, 2006. 400–412.

Russo, Richard. "The Whore's Child." *The Compact Bedford Introduction to Literature*. Ed. Michael Meyer. 7th ed. Boston: Bedford-St. Martin's, 2006. 505–515.

The Expectations of a Rose

Katherine Marchand

Assignment: In this out-of-class essay, the student was to write a literary analysis or a comparison/-contrast essay on two stories from assigned selections.

The character of Emily is illustrated in *A Rose for Emily* by William Faulkner as one of desperation, regret, and desire. This is not unlike the character of Miss Havisham in *Great Expectations* by Charles Dickens. Both authors introduce the reader to women that are jilted by their lovers and subsequently isolated from society and, more importantly, reality. This is specifically seen by the women's relationships with their fathers, their view on time, and the way the authors develop the house as a means of hiding from the breavement generated by their lost romance.

Both women have very different relationships with their fathers. Nevertheless, this first male relationship leads to the ultimate destruction of any future relationships that they may have with members of the opposite sex. Miss Emily's father is strong and domineering: "Miss Emily a slender figure in white in the background, her father a spraddled silhouette in the foreground, his back to her clutching a horsewhip, the two of them framed by the backflung front door" (Faulkner 171). He is not standing at the front door in an attempt to beat Emily with the horsewhip; rather, he is standing there to beat back any possible suitors that would consider a relationship with his daughter, the virginal lady in white. In essence, he is the overbearing patriarch that ruins any chance Emily has in finding a suitable match. She later has to deal with an unsuitable match for her position in society; nevertheless, it is a match for an old spinster. Miss Havisham's father, in contrast, is overindulgent and "denied her nothing" (Dickens 160). He certainly gives her every material possession she may need or desire. Nevertheless, this overindulgence can be seen as damaging in itself. Through this so-called love, she can never learn true comfort that is contained in the joys of a real emotional attachment. This kind of behavior towards a child can have the same results as Emily's case and is thoroughly illustrated in the novel: "'I have some sick fancies... and I have a sick fancy that I want to see some play'" (52). She lives a life that contains highly dramatic moments which is heightened further by impossibly complicated plotting. Because she is let down by every man she ever truly loved, she plots to make her adopted daughter Estella a tool against men. The tool exacts her revenge on all men since all of the men in her past have failed her; that first failure was in her father. This failure in her father is evident when he remarried and sired another son without her knowledge: "'He married his second wife privately... When she was dead...he told his first daughter what he had done, and then the son became a part of the family'" (160). The way that both of these women's fathers treat them leads to their eventual demise as women, leads to their destructive choices in future men, and illustrates their destructive choices to regain control after the men they love leave them.

Not only do both women have troubling relationships with their fathers, but they also wish to live in their pasts. Moreover, they wish to live in a time when their futures were bright and full of prospects. In order to do this, they have to hide away from the passage of time. For Emily she hides a pocket watch away from sight. The narrator states that "[she had] a thin gold chain descending to her waist and vanishing into her belt... [there was an] invisible watch ticking at the end of the gold chain" (Faulkner 170). This shows that she has turned her back on the passage of time. She wants to live in a time where her prospects were not so bleak. However, since she keeps the ticking timepiece hidden on her person, it shows that she needs the constant reminder of what has happened in her past and what could occur in her future. Miss Havisham, on the other hand, manages to rid herself of time more succinctly than Miss Emily does. She abandons any possibility of reconciling with the present by destroying time itself. Time and the passage of time are literally and symbolically destroyed by her by stopping the clock at 8:40—the time she read the note from her fiancée, Compeyson, saying that he could not marry her; therefore, "the day came, but not the bridegroom. He wrote a letter…which she received… at twenty minutes to nine" (Dickens 162). Since her perfect future is no longer available, she had resorted to living in that one moment in the past and exacting her revenge on all men through Estella. Moreover, Miss Havisham is like Miss Emily in the need to have a reminder of what has happened with time and what could occur. She does this by having all the clocks kept in place: "There was a clock in the outer wall of this house. Like the clock in Miss Havisham's room, and like Miss Havisham's watch, it had stopped at twenty minutes to nine" (71). Even though the clocks are stopped, they are still in place. If she truly wanted to lose herself in the past, not only would she have stopped the clocks, but also she would have removed them from the house.

Nevertheless, the homes that these desperate women live in can be seen as symbols of their loss. The room where Emily keeps the corpse of Homer can be at best described as a wedding tomb, and "a thin, acrid pall as of the tomb seemed to lie everywhere upon this room decked and furnished as for a bridal" (Faulkner 175). This place of rest could have been fit for a future husband because of all the gifts she had purchased for their wedding night. However, it is left as a grim reminder of what could happen with the uncontrollable forces that created havoc in her life. She has created a mausoleum for herself to weep over the loss of the only man with whom she thought that she could possibly have a proper relationship. This symbol of lost romance is locked up and hidden in a "region above the stairs which no one had seen in forty years, and which would have to be forced" (175). In the hidden room, she is able to fully realize the importance of what had happened in her past, but it also appears to be her strength to carry on. It is like a magical talisman and reminder of what destruction has occurred in her lifetime. Miss Havisham also creates a tomb for a house: "Some of the windows had been walled up; of those that remained, all the lower were rustily. There was a court-yard in front, and that was barred" (Dickens 49). However, she ensures that the entire house is the constant reminder, whereas Emily only leaves a room as her place of remembrance. Moreover, Miss Havisham carries this desire of having a place to recognize the past acts by going as far as living in the exact moment when she found out that Compeyson had jilted her. She goes as far as leaving her wedding cake exactly as it was when she found out the disastrous news; "an epergne or centerpiece of some kind was in the middle of this cloth; it was so heavily overhung with cobwebs that its form was quite undistinguishable; and, as I looked along the yellow expanse... it seaming to grow, like a black fungus" (75). She lives her life symbolically at the moment her life crashed. However, she uses her broken heart in conjunction with Estella to exact her revenge on mankind. This can be seen as worse than what Emily does as it damages far more people than just the ones directly involved.

In the end, both women use unorthodox methods in order to try to regain their lost love. "'I'll tell you... what real love is. It is blind devotion, unquestioning self-humiliation, utter submission, trust and belief against yourself and against the whole world, giving up your whole heart and soul to the smiter!'" (Dickens 215). This is exactly what both women do when they demonstrate utter love and devotion. However, they also need this real love to be reciprocated, which unfortunately cannot happen due to the men that they choose. This choice ultimately occurs because of the first male relationship with their fathers. Their regret is specifically highlighted by their feelings toward time. Their desire is shown by how they keep their houses after each traumatic deed. Through all of this, both Faulkner and Dickens show their masterful use of literary skills to create characters that show the desperation that can be borne from abandonment.

Works Cited

Dickens, Charles. *Great Expectations*. New York: The Modern Library, 2001.

Faulkner, William. "A Rose for Emily." *Literature and its Writers: A Compact Introduction to Fiction, Poetry, and Drama*. Ed. Ann and Samuel Charters. 3rd ed. Boston: Bedford, 2004. 168–175.

A Loss of Innocence

Hillary Traylor

Assignment: In this out-of-class essay, the student was to develop a character analysis.

The main character of Andre Dubus's "Killings" epitomizes the positive traits inherent to the role of a father. Through Matt Fowler's interactions with the other characters in the story, the reader is shown the internal conflict waging inside of him. The death of Fowler's son Frank serves as a catalyst for the change that will occur in him. In Matt Fowler, Dubus creates a round character that exemplifies the motives of a loving father and husband, who must make the ultimate sacrifice for his family.

Throughout the course of the story, Matt Fowler's love for his wife, Ruth, is transparent and strong. From the beginning, it is clear that Matt has a deep concern for his wife's well-being and will go to great lengths to protect her. Numerous times, he alludes to the fact that Ruth sees her son's killer (Richard Strout) and that "it's killing her" (5). Because of the pain his wife is enduring, Matt knows he must take action, even if that means he must sacrifice a part of his humanity. As the story progresses, there is a strong internal conflict raging inside of Matt that must be brought to the surface. While he is making preparations for the murder of Strout, he consistently brings up Ruth's willingness to "shoot him [Strout] herself, if she thought she could hit him" (27). This awareness serves as a reinforcement and reminder to Matt that he must take action on his wife's behalf. The relationship between Ruth and Matt is strong, and it is because of this strength that their love can transcend death and even murder. Ironically, Matt murders Richard because of his love for his wife, but ultimately this pure love will be sacrificed the moment he commits murder.

Matt Fowler's role as a father further develops his round character, and also enhances the internal conflict within him. The death of his son Frank serves as the starting point for a drastic change and psychological battle within Matt. At the death of his son, Fowler feels "all the fears he had borne...and all the grief he had been afraid of..." (77). Characteristic of a round character, Matt continually has conflicting feelings while he is carrying out the murder of Strout. Right before he begins to execute his plan to kill Strout, he has flashbacks of protecting and watching over his three children. These flashbacks serve as a reminder of why Matt is killing Strout and portray Matt's humane personality. As the kidnapping is taking place, Matt associates Richard with his son's death and grave; this connection helps him proceed with the execution. Not only does Matt feel he must protect his wife, but he also feels it is necessary to seek revenge on the "last person and thing Frank saw on earth" (93). Even after he kills Richard, Matt continues to protect his living children, instead of focusing on the pain he has experienced. Matt Fowler forces himself to keep his emotions "silent in his heart," while seeking to hide his children from the pain he has experienced (169). In the entire story, the reader can never escape the fact that Matt Fowler is a father; Dubus uses Matt's role as a father to continually remind the reader of his humanity.

In "Killings," Dubus leaves the reader with contradictory opinions concerning the actions of Matt Fowler. However, the conflicting emotions the reader feels can only graze the surface of what Matt Fowler feels throughout the story. Dubus succeeds in creating a round character, who challenges all the ideas common to a father and husband.

Works Cited

Dubus, Andre. "Killings." *The Bedford Introduction to Literature*. 6th ed. Ed. Michael Meyer. Boston: Bedford/St. Martin's, 2002. 100–112.

Interpreter of Maladies

Jennifer Simpliciano

Assignment: In this out-of-class essay, the student was to analyze a short story of his or her choice.

"Men in general are quick to believe that which they wish to be true," says Julius Caesar, a Roman leader from 49–44BC ("Quotes by: Caesar, Julius"). No other observation fits Jhumpa Lahiri's characters, Mrs. Das and Mr. Kapasi, from "Interpreter of Maladies" quite as well. Through her subtle symbolism and careful descriptions, Lahiri emphasizes one of the faults of humankind summed up simply by Julius Caesar. People will see what they want to see and hear what they want to hear. Mrs. Das refuses to acknowledge the root meaning of her emotional problems stemming from the extramarital affair which results in Bobby's conception. Likewise, Mr. Kapasi indulges in a fantasy, believing in a connection with Mrs. Das that does not exist.

Mr. Kapasi describes the Das parents as "behaving like an older brother and sister, not parents" (41). Instead of acting maturely, Mrs. Das behaves like a selfish child by "not offering her puffed rice to anyone" (40). She ignores her "motherly" duties, brushing Tina off and telling her to "[l]eave me alone...You're making me mess up" in the vexed way an older sister would (40). There also does not seem to be any difference between being a "mother" and being a "sister" in the family. Mr. Kapasi observes that Mr. Das "refer[s] to his wife by her first name when speaking to the little girl" (39). The lack of "parent" titles suggests further that Mrs. Das acts like a sibling. It is easy to see why Mr. Kapasi thought it was "hard to believe that they [the Das parents] were regularly responsible for anything other than themselves," an observation which also suggests Mrs. Das' selfish behavior (41). Her immature behavior implies her refusal to "see" what is really bothering her.

Mrs. Das' childlike behavior is not the only way Lahiri hints at her unwillingness to see the truth. Lahiri cleverly uses the expression "to shed some light on the matter" in the symbolism. For many parts of the story, Mrs. Das is "lost behind her sunglasses" (46). The sunglasses "shield" her from the truth that she refuses to see. Coincidentally, she is wearing the sunglasses when she is visiting the temple "dedicated to the great master of life, the sun…" (45). The wheels on the architecture "symbolize the wheel of life" and depict the "achievement of realization" (46). By including the description that Mrs. Das is wearing sunglasses when visiting a *sun* temple, Lahiri implies her refusal to allow any "light to be shed" on her problems that may not be what she wants to hear and her unwillingness to "achieve realization," realization that the "pain" Mrs. Das experiences is really just guilt.

The sunglasses also serve as her "window." Mrs. Das wears the sunglasses when she speaks with her family, but when she becomes interested in Mr. Kapasi and his possible ability to tell her what she wants to hear, she "lift[s] her pinkish brown sunglasses and arranged them on the top of her head like a tiara" as if to "open" the window into her sorrows (42). Her childlike behavior also "ends" to an extent when she thinks Mr. Kapasi can help her. Though refusing to share any food before, Mrs. Das happily asks Mr. Kapasi, "Would you like a piece of gum?" (42)

Unfortunately, Mr. Kapasi interprets Mrs. Das' sudden interest incorrectly, an odd coincidence as he is an interpreter. Mr. Kapasi assumes the interest to be romantic. Blinded by his own loneliness, Mr. Kapasi grows increasingly infatuated with Mrs. Das as the day goes on: "Her sudden interest in him, an interest she did not express in either her husband or her children, was mildly intoxicating" (43). He wonders "if Mr. and Mrs. Das were a bad match, just as he and his wife were" (43). With no romantic affection from his own wife, Mr. Kapasi begins to have romantic feelings towards Mrs. Das, feelings that he assures himself are reciprocal. He argues that Mrs. Das curiously "used the word 'romantic'" to describe Mr. Kapasi, but "did not behave in a romantic way toward her husband" (43).

Caught up in his fantasy, Mr. Kapasi continuously misinterprets the interaction between himself and Mrs. Das. Mrs. Das asks for his address to send pictures, but instead of taking the request for what it was (just a request), Mr. Kapasi interprets it as an invitation for further communication. He writes his address in "clear, careful letters" and envisions "respond[ing] eloquently…" (45). He hopes that Mrs. Das will confess the "disappointment of her marriage" and his friendship with her "would grow, and flourish" (45). After he gives back the slip of paper with his address, he becomes distressed, "worried that he had either misspelled his name, or accidentally reversed the numbers of his postal code" (45). He even calculates the approximate time it would take for her to respond. He does not notice that Mrs. Das does not find further communication a priority, dropping the paper "into the jumble of her bag" instead of keeping it more carefully in a wallet (45).

Interestingly, Mr. Kapasi plans to hide the picture of Mrs. Das and him "safely tucked between the pages of his Russian grammar" (45). Mr. Kapasi, whose dream it was to become a great interpreter of nations, does not remember Russian anymore. Lahiri suggests that Mr. Kapasi wishes for a secret relationship with Mrs. Das, but does not understand, or refuses to see, the real meaning of Mrs. Das' interest in him like he does not understand the meaning of Russian words.

After their talk in the car, both Mr. Kapasi and Mrs. Das realize that they were kidding themselves, but Mrs. Das does not give up without a fight. She pleads with Mr. Kapasi to "say the right thing," in other words, say something that she wants to hear. Mr. Kapasi, however, says the very truth that Mrs. Das has been shielding herself from: that she feels not real pain, but guilt. Mr. Kapasi eventually grasps the reality of his "relationship" with her after the piece of paper with his address floats away in the air.

With these two characters, Lahiri makes it clear to the readers that believing in something because they want it to be true will not do any good for anybody and effectively warns readers of Julius Caesar's unfortunate truth: "Men willingly believe what they wish" ("Quotes by: Caesar, Julius").

Works Cited

Lahiri, Jhumpa. "Interpreter of Maladies." *Literature: An Introduction to Fiction, Poetry, and Drama*. Ed. Joseph Terry et al. 4th ed. Taunton: Quebecor World, 2005. 37–52.

"Quotes by: Caesar, Julius." *Quotations Book*. 2007. 6 May 2007 <http://www.quotationsbook.com/author/1234/>.

The Sacrifice

Dee Stephens

Assignment: In this out-of-class assignment, the student was to discuss a specific aspect of an assigned literary work.

In James Balwin's "Sonny's Blues," the narrator sacrifices a great deal by returning to Harlem. He thinks he had done the right thing and that it is the only thing to do. He worked hard to become someone who could give back to the community from which he had come. However, his younger brother, Sonny, struggles with heroin addiction and dreams of becoming a musician. Their differences are a constant rift between the two. Surprisingly, in the end, it is Sonny who demonstrates the greatest love, compassion, and understanding for his people.

Harlem, at the time of the story, is a community of poverty, violence, oppression, and darkness. Music plays a large role in escaping the "killing streets" (311). The narrator seems to notice this for the first time on the day he is faced with his brother's drug charges. To his confusion, one of his students, who has every reason to be "filled with rage," is "whistling a tune" (305). The tune "seemed to be pouring out of him as though he were a bird," though the "harsh" setting hardly provides one with reason to sing (305). Later, as the narrator walks the streets of the despairing community, he is drawn to a bar where the juke box is playing something "black and bouncy" (307). The music seems to have a magical effect on the barmaid working there. While the music plays, she is full of life and laughter. "When she smiled, one saw the little girl," but when the music stopped, "one sensed the doomed, still-struggling woman beneath the battered face of the semi-whore" (307). For many people in Harlem, music is freedom. Music could carry them away to a better place—a place not yet realized by Sonny's brother.

The two brothers struggle with their grim existence in their own way, though they both have the need to escape their menacing reality (307). When confronted with the news of Sonny's arrest, the narrator "hadn't wanted to know" (304). His way of coping is denial. However, while walking the streets of Harlem with a childhood friend of Sonny's, the narrator is forced to look at his brother, his community, and himself in a way that he refused to see in the past. His company may have well been his conscience, as the man poses questions he did not want to hear. After struggling with his conflicting emotions, the narrator decides that it is not his business and chooses to push all thoughts of his brother aside (308). After all, he has done his part. He is a responsible father and husband. He has chosen to return to Harlem with his family to be of service to his community, and he has done all he could do for Sonny.

Sonny has a different way of coping with his bleak surroundings. As a boy, he first turns to music to escape his darkness. He develops an almost obsessive passion for the piano. When Sonny played, "it was as though he were all wrapped up in some cloud, some fire, some vision all his own; and there wasn't any way to reach him" (321). When he learned that his substitute family considered his music unbearable, it was as though "they [had] penetrated his cloud" (321). He gave up on his music for a time and tried to escape Harlem by joining the navy. After Sonny's return from the navy, there was a big change in his behavior. His older brother began to notice Sonny's dreamlike state. He did not approve of his younger brother's friends, and Sonny's music had become just another part of his destructive lifestyle (322). Instead of being constructively consumed by music, Sonny had become lost in his heroin addiction.

It is not until he feels the deep pain of losing a child that the narrator begins to empathize and connect with Sonny (323). When he reaches out to Sonny in prison, he is received with compassion that he himself had not shown by deserting his brother during his time of need (309). There is more to learn after Sonny's homecoming. The narrator has not understood what Sonny knows all along about music—how it can "cease lamenting" (332). And for perhaps the first time in his life, he listens to his younger brother as he tells of the *"repulsive"* suffering involved when artists share their pain (326). As he later listens to Sonny play, the narrator finally feels the freedom Sonny offers in his music, and he knows his brother risked "ruin, destruction, madness, and death, in order to find new ways to make [him] listen" (332).

The narrator begins to realize that perhaps his sacrifice is not as significant as he once thought. It is true enough that he has given his time and hard work to become a teacher in his community. Sonny, however, knows that people need more than education to survive in Harlem. They need to connect from within and to share their pain. They need something to get lost in. Sonny has given them that—something that may give them a moment of true freedom from the darkness and suffering around them. Through his own pain, he has taken the burden of his people and placed it on his back, and that is the greatest sacrifice of all.

Works Cited

Baldwin, James. "Sonny's Blues." *40 Short Stories. A Portable Anthology.* Ed. Beverly Lawn. 2nd ed. Boston: New York—St. Martin's, 2004. 304–333.

Water Symbolism in Morrison's Beloved

Dennis Devlin

Assignment: In this out-of-class researched essay, the student was to discuss a specific literary element in the novel Beloved.

Symbolism enriches literature by representing a larger, more significant idea. Throughout the novel *Beloved*, Toni Morrison uses numerous symbols to give the reader a greater insight into the complexity of her characters. More specifically, Morrison uses the motif of water, in many of its traditional symbolic forms, to represent birth, rebirth, and escape to freedom, as she weaves a haunting tale of the slavery experience in America.

According to the University of Michigan's online *Dictionary of Symbolism*, water is a conventional representation of life. It can be associated with birth, fertility, and refreshment. In a Christian context, according to Tressider, water has numerous correlations. Christ walked on water and transformed it into wine; thus such acts can be seen as a "transcendence of the earthly condition" (222). Christians are baptized with or in water, symbolizing a purification of the soul—and an admission into the faith. Flood myths in which a sinful society is destroyed are examples of cleansing and regeneration symbolism (Tressider 222). The online *Dictionary of Symbolism* further describes the symbolic associations of water as follows: "Water is one of the four elements essential to life in traditional western philosophy. Its qualities are fluidity and cohesiveness. Flowing water, like a river, usually represents change and the passage of time." Water still offers powerful symbolism within the overall realm of imaginative experience, particularly as it mirrors internal states and emotions.

In the novel *Beloved*, the scene involving Sethe and Amy Denver at the river offers the use of water as a traditional symbol of birth and new life. As Sethe gets close to the river, "her own water broke loose to join it. The break, followed by the redundant announcement of labor, arched her back" (83). Unable to think of "anywhere to go but in," Sethe "crawled into the boat" that soon began to fill with water, and with the compassionate assistance of the runaway indentured servant, Amy Denver, gave birth to her daughter, whom she names Denver.

The appearance of the white girl signals the creation of a new family, and although Sethe and Amy "never expected to see each other again in this world," they "couldn't care less" because "there on a summer night surrounded by bluefern they did something together appropriately and well. A patroller passing would have sniggered to see two throw-away people, two lawless outlaws—a slave and a barefoot white woman with unpinned hair—wrapping a ten-minute-old baby in rags they wore" (84–85). When Sethe names her baby after Amy Denver, she acknowledges Amy as kin, responsible for Denver's birth (Heinze 94). The fact that the birth occurs at the river in a boat full of water lends powerful creation and life imagery to the experience, and the characters emerge reconstructed as fully human, not as objectified slaves.

Morrison constructs another image of rebirth in the scene where Beloved emerges from the water, like a child born from a watery sac. In this passage, Beloved, the daughter that Sethe murdered eighteen years ago, presumably comes back to the world of the living. When Beloved first appears at Sethe's house, Sethe leans in to look at the strange woman, and "the moment she got close enough to see the face," she suddenly feels a great need to relieve herself; "She never made the outhouse. Right in front of its door she had to lift her skirts and the water she voided was endless. Like a horse, she thought, but as it went on and on she thought, 'No, more like flooding the boat when Denver was born'" (50). When Sethe looks at Beloved's face, her bladder fills up. Significantly, Sethe thinks the endless turret of water is similar to the "flooding" that took place at the time of Denver's birth (Samuels 122). The symbolic breaking of water Sethe experiences when she sees Beloved on the stump, combined with the act of Beloved emerging from the water, provides compelling imagery of the delivery process, or in this case, the rebirthing process, and the moment concludes years of Sethe's dreaming of her baby girl, killed by Sethe's own hand, now seemingly reborn into the world.

Water is again used as a motif that signifies rebirth further on in the novel, but this time in reference to Sethe, representing more of an act of cleansing or purification. When Sethe arrives at Baby Suggs' home, she is met by Baby Suggs, who takes it upon herself to wash and bathe Sethe's body: "[Baby Suggs] led Sethe to the keeping room and, by the light of a spirit lamp, bathed her in sections, starting with her face. Then, while waiting for another pan of heated water, she sat next to her and stitched cotton. Sethe dozed and woke to the washing of her hands and arms . . . the rest of the night Sethe spent soaking" (93). In this scene, Sethe has just arrived at Baby Suggs' home in Cincinnati after making her escape from Sweet Home, having been molested by school-teacher's nephews and also having given birth to Denver. Sethe was clearly soiled, both physically and emotionally, and she needed to be bathed and cleansed. Baby Suggs bathes her, providing the "ritual purifi-cation (rebirth) that Sethe needs to enter the new community of freed slaves" (Samuels 122).

For Paul D., water was a fundamental part of obtaining his free-dom from the prison camps in Alfred, Georgia. Morrison writes of Paul D.'s ordeal: "It rained. In the boxes the men heard the water rise in the trench and looked out for cottonmouths. They squatted in muddy water, slept above it, peed in it . . . it happened so quick he had no time to ponder . . . one by one, from Hi Man back on down the line, they dove. Down through the mud under the bars, blind, groping" (110). In this passage, Paul D. is locked up and chained with all the other prisoners.

One day it starts to rain and does not stop, raining so much that all the dirt under the bars of the "cells" turned to soft mud. At this point, the prisoners decide to escape, diving through the mud and run-ning away to safety and freedom. According to Tressider, "the purest waters—especially dew and spring water, but also rain—are thought to have numinous and curative properties as forms of divine grace, gifts of Mother Earth (spring water) or sky gods (rain and dew)" (223). Surely the sky gods looked down upon Paul D. that day, blessing him with the gift of rain that would grant him his escape to freedom and new life.

Water represents liberty for Sethe as well. In order to get away from schoolteacher and slavery, it is necessary for her to cross the Ohio River, a large body of water. Once she crosses it to the land of freedom, she has new life (Samuels 122). In this passage, Sethe has just delivered

Denver, her baby, when she runs into Stamp Paid and two boys. Stamp Paid takes her across the river because he knows that someone will be waiting on the other side to help her. Once again, Morrison makes the connection between water and new life, and Sethe's crossing of the river symbolizes her escape from Sweet Home and slavery.

Another illustration of this idea may be found in the incident concerning Sethe, Denver, and Paul D.'s first encounter with the mysterious young woman, Beloved, who, after being offered water by Denver, cannot seem to satiate her thirst. Morrison writes: "Four times Denver filled it, and four times the woman drank as though she had crossed a desert" (51). According to some interpretations, the desert may not be that of sand, but of an ocean crossed by the slaves aboard the slave ships, a passage during which they were forbidden water due to short supplies. Beloved's need for water throughout the book, then, may signify "not only the thirst for water the future slaves suffered, but also the thirst for freedom they must have longed for" (*Symbolism and Images*).

Morrison continually returns to a water motif that is dominant in *Beloved*, associated particularly with Sethe, the main character. Morrison clearly makes the connection between water and life, as well as rebirth and freedom, in order to demonstrate how each person in the novel is able to transcend his or her current earthly conditions and aspire to new hope and freedom. What we learn from Morrison's extraordinary style and clever use of symbolism touches us at a level deeper than simple understanding.

Works Cited

Dictionary of Symbolism. University of Michigan. Originally Constructed by Allison Protas. Augmented and refined by Geoff Brown and Jamie Smith in 1997 and by Eric Jaffe in 2001. <*http://www.umich.edu/~umfandsf/symbolismproject/symbolism.html/*>

Heinze, Denise. *The Dilemma of Double Consciousness: Toni Morrison's Novels.* Athens: University of Georgia Press, 1993.

Morrison, Toni. *Beloved.* New York: Plume, 1988.

Samuels, Wilfred. *Toni Morrison.* New York: Twayne Publisher, 1990.

Symbolism and Images. Beloved Study Guide. Oregon State University. 21 July 2002. <http://www.web.cocc.edu/wr316ca/beloved/symbolism.htm>.

Tressider, Jack. *Dictionary of Symbols: An Illustrated Guide to Traditional Images, Icons and Emblems.* San Francisco: Chronicle Books, 1998.

Life's Journeys

Pamela D. Azar

Assignment: Using a reader-response approach, the student was to use the language of a short story to explore experiences in her own life.

I pulled out of my driveway without headlights so as not to awaken my parents or any nosey neighbors. With a little shove from my brothers, Trey and Brooks, I was off and rolling at three o'clock on a dreadfully chilly winter morning. I can still remember the sound of the dead pine needles and tiny rocks cracking under my tires in the silence of the night. I can still see my brothers' pink faces through my rearview mirror as they struggled to push me down the street so that I could jump-start my bright yellow 1976 Volkswagen Super Beetle. These were the remembrances mistfully meandering through my mind as I read Louise Erdrich's "The Red Convertible" (161–168). My journey greatly resembles that of Lyman and Henry Lamartine as they travel up long stretches of highway and down rigorous roads of life.

I was seventeen years old, and like Lyman, I "could always make money" (161). Even before I was legally able to work, my brothers and I would haul a lawnmower, a wheel barrel, a rake and some trash bags around the neighborhood to see if we could cut people's grass. We would charge $10 for small yards, $15 for medium yards, and $20 for big yards. We usually averaged about $60 a-piece, and when we were done spending that, we would cut more grass. I had my first job when I was sixteen at Pizza Hut on Spring

Street which is on the outskirts of downtown Macon, Georgia. I am
sure that Lyman's job ("washing dishes at the Joliet Café") was more
blissful then serving coffee to homeless bums, and beer to already
inebriated party goers (161). I could only put up with that kind of
thing for so long, and so, about two months later I got another job
delivering pizzas for Papa John's Pizza on Tom Hill Sr. Blvd. That
was the perfect job for me. I loved to drive. Even after work my
brothers and I would go driving around the streets of Macon, smoke
pot, laugh, munch on Cheetos, and laugh and laugh. We always
went home late in the evenings because, by then Joe and Mom
would have stopped arguing about whatever, and there would be
peace in the house. They were always screaming at each other. Joe
is my step-father, and Trey and Brooks were his boys, but it never
occurred to me to call them "step-brothers" because we were as
close as Lyman and Henry were before Henry went off to war and
before "the enemy caught him" (163). That would be the routine for
an entire year until that next autumn.

I really do not know how it all came about. I remember a huge
fight in the house, and I ran out and went to Freedom Park (where
I played softball), and I sat there and cried. Then, I remember feeling a strong breeze, and I noticed the coldness of the tears on my
face. I could hear children playing in the distance on the nearby
playground. "Why had I come here?" I thought. *Freedom* Park, and
in that instant, as the leaves were rustling in the wind, I knew I had
to get away from my house. As I inhaled a deep breath of air, a smile
came over my face, and the plan started to form in my mind. As
I was sitting there, I felt like Lyman in his description:

> I do remember this one place with willows. I remember I laid
> under those trees and it was comfortable. So comfortable. The
> branches bent down all around me like a tent or a stable. And
> quiet, it was quiet, even though there was a powwow close
> enough so I could see it going on. The air was not too still,
> not too windy either [. . .] I feel good. (162)

I felt good, too, and in some way, that was a freeing moment in
itself.

I had an older half-sister, Cindy, in Texas. She went to live
with her dad when she was sixteen. She had always been somewhat
of a wild child and a party lover. She was irresponsible and had a dis-
turbingly dependent nature. I now partially blame this on her father

who never knew how to discipline her and bailed her out of every type of trouble she got into. His love for her was measured with the amount of money he gave to her, but who was complaining? She got pregnant when she was eighteen, and she married two months before the baby was due at the ripe old age of nineteen. Before my journey took place, she would have two more children by two more men, all three of whom were abusive. I knew of her little bouts with cocaine and alcohol, but I had spent the summer with her that year, and she just drank beer. There were never any drugs around.

Georgia law says, in not so many words, that it is legal for a minor of seventeen years of age to leave his or her house without the permission of the parents. So, two weeks after my seventeenth birthday, I did just that. The decision to go that very moment was somewhat spontaneous although I had written the *Goodbye* letter weeks before. It was marked with dried teardrops. This type of spontaneity comes along with youth, which is very important when trying to understand the mindsets of Lyman and Henry the day they meet Susy (a hitchhiker) and offer her a ride home:

> "Hop on in," says Henry. So she climbs in between us.
> "We'll take you home," I [Lyman] says. "Where do you live?"
> "Chicken," she says.
> "Where the hell's that?" I ask her.
> "Alaska."
> "Okay," says Henry, and we drive. (162)

Their highways and byways were much longer than my own, but held similar purpose.

I was on my way to Houston, Texas, a new life, a new start, and a big city. I craved freedom, and I had somewhere to be other than Macon, Georgia. I was the first child in the household to own a car, and "Canary" (my pet name for my Bug) and I had a great distance to fare. I had never made that trip alone. My mom and I would always go during the summer. We would pack a cooler and our suitcases and drive 850 miles to see Cindy and the children. We would always sing along with the radio, or if we tired of listening to the new stuff, we would sing oldies like "Abba Dabba Honeymoon" and "Elvira." We loved to sing and laugh. I think it was our own way of escaping the everyday mental torments of the house. I missed her, but youthful delusions of grandeur drove me ever forward.

With the chill of the night came tears. There was not much to see through those tears, at night, except the flickers of oncoming bugs reflecting in the headlights of my car. However, when the sun rose, as I was heading out of Montgomery, Alabama, towards Mississippi. I felt a tingling warmth come over me, and I could do nothing but smile. Interstate 10 is the main highway that goes from Mississippi through Texas. Along the way are huge bridges over bayous and swamplands. I can remember always looking for alligators in the swamps passing by as a child. Crossing the Mississippi is a wondrous sight to see. There are always huge barges drifting around the ports, but the bridge is so high they look like snap-together model boats you would put together as a child. In Louisiana there is an eleven mile long bridge that spans one of the largest swamps in the United States, and after that there is the St. Charles River which is lined with casinos and fancy hotels. The huge casino riverboats with the big spinning paddle-wheels on the back of them would float around in the bays. I now wonder what scenes Lyman beheld as he traveled through "Spokane and across Idaho then Montana [. . .] under the Canadian border through Columbus, DesLacs [. . . and] Bottineau County" (163). This trip, however, I would hardly notice any of these things, for I was alone and focused solely on the road ahead of me.

I was free from my little world of hell. I felt like Lyman seemed to feel when he said, "You never feel like you have to sleep hard or put away the world" (162). I no longer had the stresses of my parents' constant arguing and bickering pressed upon me, nor did I have to be the proverbial "shoulder" for my mother to cry on after it was all said and done. It seemed harsh to feel that way, but after so many years of misery, it became mentally exhausting. When I arrived, Cindy and the children greeted me at the door with smiles and hugs which, by that time, I was craving. This was going to be great. I would enroll into a public high school as a transfer student and graduate and go to college and do the things I was supposed to do without the supervision of my parents. Well, I started out that way, but the second week in *public* high school proved to be menial to me, the overqualified Catholic schoolgirl. The "kids," as I called them, couldn't hold a conversation with a rock and loved to spread full course meals on their desks during class. If any of my teachers said anything, I would never have a clue due to the yapping and laughing as the wads of paper would dart across the room. What a nightmare! Needless to say, I dropped out and became a great pothead.

The only people I had to hide my weed from now were Cindy's children, and even if they *did* find it, what trouble would I get into? Cindy had never grown up and, although she was ten years older than I, she was not at all mature. She was always the person who could find any drug that anybody wanted. She worked as a cocktail waitress at a gentlemen's cabaret called Paradise. She had a plethora of customers including the exotic dancers. It was not until about two months later that I found out about her very well concealed cocaine habit. I had often wondered how she stayed up to all hours of the morning and could still walk around after a case or so of beer. Of course I was stoned and drunk most of the time as well, and although I considered myself to be wise beyond my years, I was still a bit naïve when it came to the world of *hard* drugs. Though soon, I would come to lose that aspect of childhood innocence as well. Warm nights, lots of drugs, strippers from the club, other friends of mine, and good music were all part of a normal evening at home for the two of us. My freedom soon became my captor. Spring soon became a haze passing as quickly as a good night's sleep.

Summer was in the midst, and I was going nowhere. My heart was telling me that this was all wrong. One day I was at a friend's house, and we decided to drop acid. It just so happened, with that particular "trip," a great revelation came to mind (along with the pretty colors) that I would go home and in doing so, escape the greater hell than that from which I came. Homeward bound it was for Canary and me. My pace was slower on the way back. I was relaxed and happy, and I noticed everything from the damaged roads of Louisiana and the little blue emergency call boxes on the right side of the eleven mile bridge to the Tuskegee Airmen Historical Site in Alabama to the big "Welcome to Georgia" sign in Columbus. I knew I was a changed person, but I was glad to be home.

At first I was very similar to Lyman's description of Henry as he says, "[. . .] Henry was different, and I'll say this: the change was no good" (164). I had no idea of how to act around my family, especially my mother. The guilt for having left her was eating away at me. I had been gone for nearly six months, and I had talked to her very little because she laid guilt on top of guilt, and it hurt. I tried talking with her about why I left and why I came back. She listened, but in her mind it was something I should never have done, and in my mind, I knew that it was something that had to be done. Now we both know that, had I not gone to Houston, we would never have known about Cindy.

Mom had no idea of what a world full of drugs is like. She was the girl next door and a devout Christian. It was up to me to let her know what the other side looks like, so I told her my story. We cried together, and we realized that we had to get Cindy home. We tried talking; we then asked her to seek counseling, and Mom finally went as far as having her picked up and taken to a rehabilitation facility. Nothing worked. We talked to psychologists who said to use tough love. We talked to pastors and priests who said to pray. Then Mom and I finally talked to each other and decided to go get her and the children, and they came back with us. They stayed at the house for about a month, but Cindy never did get along with mom, so she moved out. Unfortunately, sometime after that, she figured out that people in Macon sell drugs, too, and her addictions got the better of her. So many nights I chased her into the dark corners of cracktown only to find a sullen skeleton of a sister. She had changed even more than I. She resembled Henry when Lyman said, "[. . .] he was quiet, so quiet, and never comfortable sitting still anywhere, but always up and moving around" (164). She could not sit through a movie without getting up at least five times to do something or another. There were times when I felt like screaming at her like Lyman did with Henry the night they went down to the river and '[he] took Henry by the shoulders and started shaking him. "Wake up," I says, "wake up, wake up, wake up'" (166). I wanted her to come back to reality and just stop doing drugs. In the world of addiction, however, that is easier said than done.

She moved back to Texas a few years later only to follow the same path she had taken for so many years. She is 36 years old now and has finally stopped doing drugs. It took me a year to believe her because, normally, addicts are habitual liars, and she had proven that theory to me time and time again. Seeing is believing, however, so Mom and I made the trip to Houston to visit. She had transformed like Henry when Lyman says, "his face looked to me as if it was clear, more peaceful" (166). It was a difficult journey for all of us. Cindy and I fought with our rivers and were fortunate enough to have come across them without having our "boots filled" (161).

Works Cited

Erdrich, Louise. "The Red Convertible." *Literature and Its Writers: A Compact Introduction to Fiction, Poetry, and Drama*. Ed. Ann Charters, et al. Boston: Bedford/ St. Martins, 2004. 161–168.

The Significance of Heritage in "Everyday Use"

Arabella Rios

Assignment: In this out-of-class assignment, the student was to discuss a specific element in an assigned short story.

Alice Walker's "Everyday Use" depicts the significance of heritage within a family. Heritage defines who we are and how we live our lives. This is what Walker tries to demonstrate throughout this story. Utilizing characterization, Walker illustrates three views through which individuals can perceive their heritage. Mama, Maggie, and Dee represent her perception of the differing ways in which an individual can express his or her heritage. Mama and Maggie honor their heritage, while Dee flaunts it.

Mama is described as a large woman who has spent most of her life working with her hands. She is not educated, but was able to maintain a home for her daughters. Walker demonstrates how Mama views her heritage by letting us know that she can trace Dee's name through her family. Mama states, "Though in fact, I probably could have carried it back beyond the Civil War through the branches" (533). It is clear that Mama knows her family's linage. Furthermore, we see Mama's encounter with Dee and the quilts. Mama knows where each piece of cloth on the quilts originates. This shows her knowledge and love for her heritage. As Mama explains to Dee that she has promised the quilts to Maggie, we can clearly devise Mama's perspective of heritage: "God knows I been saving [them] for long enough with nobody using [them]. I hope she will" (535). Mama wants her daughter Maggie to be able to use the quilts and enjoy them. She believes the quilts are for usage. Here, we clearly understand without a doubt Mama's perspective of heritage. We understand that Mama is living her heritage. She wants to be sure that her family heritage will continue well after she has "past-on." Mama knows that Maggie will carry-on; and will teach future generations about those who came before her.

Like Mama, Maggie identifies with her heritage through honor and respect. Walker informs us, "Maggie knows how to quilt" (535). This conveys that Maggie has learned a skill that has been a tradition in her family, a skill that can be traced through many generations in her family. In addition, Walker reveals Maggie's recollection of each family member and his / her contribution to the items in Mama's house. Maggie says, "Aunt Dee's first husband whittled the dash," and "His name was Henry, but they called him Stash" (534). It is apparent that Maggie holds her heritage in her heart. Her resolution to give the quilts to Dee proves this: "I can [re] member Grandma Dee without the quilts" (535). Contrarily, Dee does not comprehend the true content of the quilts. Even with the quilts, she would not be able to remember her ancestors.

Dee has a superficial view of her heritage. She chooses what she likes about her heritage, and she leaves out what inconveniences her. Truly, this is visible when Dee changes her name to Wangero. Dee explains, "I couldn't bear it any longer being named after the people who oppress me" (533). She is rejecting her family by rejecting her name. Dee dislikes her name as much as she dislikes Mama and Maggie. Moreover, Dee views the significance of heritage in objects. We can see this when she asks Mama for the churn top and dasher: "I can use the churn top as a centerpiece for the alcove table, and I'll think of something artistic to do with the dasher" (534). It is evident that she also perceives the quilts in the same manner. Dee refers to the quilts, "But they're priceless!" She continues, "Maggie can't appreciate these quilts," and "She'd probably be backward enough to put them to everyday use" (535). Dee is unaware of the fact that she is the one who does not appreciate the churn top, dasher, and quilts for what they are. They are not museum pieces, or objects for admiration. Dee rejects her family, but deems her family's belongings as something by which others can admirer her for. Dee regards heritage as something for displaying rather then having it become a part of her everyday life.

Heritage molds our individuality, and it reflects itself throughout our daily lives. "Everyday use" depicts this by showing how the main characters in the story view heritage. It is clear that heritage cannot be superficial. There is no purpose in collecting items that may become old and wasted if we do not comprehend their true meaning or their true origin. We must be proud of our family and ancestors to embrace fully our heritage.

Works Cited

Walker, Alice. "Everyday Use." *Literature and its Writers: A Compact Introduction to Fiction, Poetry, and Drama.* Ed. Ann and Samuel Charters. 3rd ed. Boston: Bedford, 2004. 530–536.

A Voice in the Darkness

Monica Webb Thomas

Assignment: In this out-of-class essay, the student was to analyze a short story of her choice. The use of secondary sources was optional.

Most Americans associate the Civil Rights Movement with the sixties; however, the African-American struggle for equality spans the history of the United States. One of the most important periods in this movement occurred around the time of World War II. World War II provided unprecedented opportunities for African-Americans in the civilian work force as well as in the military; however, they received less than equal treatment. This unfair treatment led to the organization of groups who demanded equal rights for workers and desegregated armed forces (Blum 756). These organizations, which emphasized nonviolent protests, became examples to other groups that were forming at the time. The war years brought continued protest, both peaceful and violent. After the war black Americans were impatient to end the official sanction of segregation as well as other exploitative policies. In order to fight these racial injustices, African-Americans turned to the courts. The fifties saw the reversal of segregation and the first civil rights legislation since the Reconstruction era (Blum 825). The advances of the forties and fifties set the stage for the Black Revolution of the sixties.

It was during the revolutionary times of the forties that James Baldwin grew to adulthood in the impoverished slums of Harlem. Upon graduating from high school, he decided to become a writer.

The newly emerging civil rights movement found literary support in his works. In the fifties he became the literary spokesman for African-Americans as well as becoming well-known for his talent in expressing the feelings and attitudes of black Americans. After living in Paris for several years, he returned to the United States and became active in the civil rights movement (Beatty 790). During this time period, Baldwin wrote a short story called "Sonny's Blues." On the surface "Sonny's Blues" is the story of two brothers: Sonny, who is struggling to overcome a drug addiction, and Sonny's brother, who tries to understand Sonny's struggle while feeling guilty for ignoring Sonny's problem. However, "Sonny's Blues" is more than a story of Sonny's drug addiction. "Sonny's Blues" describes the struggle by African-Americans to overcome oppression in the United States during the infancy of the civil rights movement.

Baldwin presents the oppression endured by African-Americans during the twenties and thirties through Sonny's mother and father. Sonny's father illustrates the dispirited hopelessness felt by this generation of African-Americans when he says, "Safe, hell! Ain't no place safe for kids, nor nobody" (Baldwin 412). The story told by Sonny's mother of Sonny's uncle's death gives insight into the racial injustices endured by this generation as well as insight into the source of their hopelessness. Baldwin also relates the opportunities for advancement this era offered by describing Sonny's father as "always on the look out for 'something a little better,' but he died before he found it" (Baldwin 412). Sonny's mother sums up the hopelessness this generation has about both the past and the future when she relates, "the world ain't changed much" (Baldwin 415). Baldwin makes it clear that African-Americans of this era felt powerless to emerge from their persecution.

Sonny and his brother represent the younger generation of African-Americans who are struggling to break free from the persecution endured by their parents. The battle of the brothers to escape Harlem depicts their generation's struggle to escape oppression. The mere fact that the brothers considered escape possible shows an expansion in opportunity because escape was not possible for black Americans in their parents' generation. Both brothers do manage to escape the "killing streets of childhood" (Baldwin 411), but they escape in vastly different ways. Sonny's brother escapes Harlem by conforming to the established government system. He joins the army, gets an education, and becomes a teacher. He lives in a housing project similar to the neighborhood he grew up in. Sonny, however, attempts to escape Harlem by rebelling. He turns to music to gain freedom, but when this fails, he turns to drugs and leaves Harlem when he is sent to prison. The irony of the brothers' escape is that neither brother really finds freedom. When they escaped oppression, there was no better place for them to go. The world had not changed much from the time of the brothers' parents. The freedom from persecution Sonny and his brother are seeking did not exist in America during the forties and fifties.

At the end of the story, Baldwin uses Sonny's struggle to play his music to summarize the struggle of African-Americans to gain equality. The passage begins, "when Creole stepped forward to remind them that they were playing the blues" (Baldwin 428). The blues is the music of the oppressed and represents the oppressed. Then Baldwin describes Sonny's music as "not about anything new" and talks of the boys "keeping it new at the risk of ruin, destruction, madness, and death in order to find new ways to make us listen" (428). Baldwin is describing the struggle for equality and emphasizing the need to keep fighting to make people hear and not ignore the injustices because the only "light" in the "darkness" of oppression is the voice struggling to "tell the tale" to the world (428). Sonny's music tells of freedom for African-Americans if America would only listen and understand the need for equality.

"Sonny's Blues" tells the tale of generations of African-Americans as they struggle to throw off the chains of oppression. Baldwin, writing from his own social experiences, illustrates the people behind a dynamic period of social awakening. In "Sonny's Blues" Baldwin makes his voice heard. He presents to us the past and the present of oppression and offers hope for a future where everyone is free and equal. The battle for equality that began in the forties continues today as a new generation attempts to make its voice heard.

Works Cited

Baldwin, James. "Sonny's Blues." *The Heath Guide to Literature*. Ed. David Bergman et al. 3rd ed. Lexington: D.C. Heath and Company, 1992. 405–429.

Beatty, Jerome, ed. *The Norton Introduction to Fiction*. New York: W.W. Norton & Company, 1996.

Blum, John M., et al. *The National Experience: Part Two: A History of the United States Since 1865*. 8th ed. Fort Worth: Harcourt Brace Jovanovich, Inc., 1993.

Blessings of a White Elephant

Connie McMeans

Assignment: In a paper written out of class, the student was to use class discussion as a point of departure in analyzing the significance of setting in an assigned short story.

In our class discussion of the story "Hills Like White Elephants" by Ernest Hemingway, we explored the meaning of the phrase "white elephant." The fact that it represents a gift that one might not find appealing significantly contributes to the story, as Jig and the American have an "unwanted gift" in their lives. By using the hills to represent the "unwanted gift" in the lives of the American and Jig, the author could be making the point that having an abortion is like removing a necessary part of nature. Even though at first glance the hills do not appear to be of any value, removing them would greatly add to the emptiness of the country and severely reduce the variety of the scenery. The hills, along with the desert and valley, entice Jig to consider the potential happiness and fulfillment that her child could bring into her life.

The story takes place at a train station in the middle of a desert. On one side of the station there are hills like white elephants, surrounded by barren country. On the other side of the station is the Ebro River, lined with trees and fields of grain. While waiting for the train to come, Jig looks out at the hills. She finds them intriguing and white, which is in total contrast to the brown, dull country surrounding the hills. The setting of the desert is appropriate because it symbolizes both the present emptiness in Jig's life as well as her potential to be fulfilled as a parent. A child would increase Jig's enjoyment of life, just as the hills naturally enhance the drab countryside. Without the hills the country would be completely expressionless, much like Jig's life would be if she chose to abort the baby. Her unwanted or unexpected child may seem to be a burden now, but, like the scenery, her child would bring increased value and purpose to her life. If she chooses to abort the child, she would be missing out on a wonderful part of life that was never meant to be discarded. Just as the desert would be empty without the hills, so her life would be barren without the baby.

As Jig later walks to the other end of the station and looks out at the Ebro, it is as if she finds the connection that nature suggests. The luscious, inviting scenery by the river is compared to the joy and fulfillment that a child could bring into her life. The prosperity of the land can be compared to the success and growth that Jig could experience if she chooses to keep her child. The purpose of paralleling the Ebro River to the hills seems to indicate that accepting the hills in a lifeless place would lead to a deeper appreciation for the beautiful Ebro River scenery. If Jig chooses to keep the baby, the baby would prove to be a starting point of life in her present state of emptiness. The possibilities that could come from keeping her child, instead of aborting him or her, are displayed through the luscious beauty of the Ebro. The river points to the child as a giver of life. If Jig chooses to keep the baby, then her life would have the potential richness shown by the Ebro.

The hills, Ebro River, and train station are obviously the perfect setting for the story. If the characters had been in another place, I doubt that Jig would have had the time or the resources of nature to reflect on her decision about having an abortion. The setting seems to oppose abortion by emphasizing the beauty that nature brings. And since having a child is a natural and wonderful part of life, aborting the child would greatly reduce Jig's potential for having a meaningful and fulfilled existence.

Works Cited

Hemingway, Ernest. "Hills Like White Elephants." *Responding to Literature.* Ed. Judith A. Stanford. Mountain View, CA: Mayfield, 1992. 986–989.

The Role of Setting in "*Araby*" and in Angela's Ashes: A Memoir

Lauren Thornton

Assignment: In this out-of-class essay, the student was asked to analyze an assigned literary work.

When most people think of Ireland, they think of a lush, green countryside and quaint farm cottages. After all, Ireland is known as the Emerald Isle. However, all of Ireland is not so beautiful and green. The cities in Ireland can be quite harsh, especially for the poor. It is this harsher side of Ireland that James Joyce, author of "Araby," and Frank McCourt, author of *Angela's Ashes: A Memoir*, describe for their readers. The authors take the reader to the poverty-stricken streets of Ireland where the desolate setting symbolizes the dismal lives that the narrators of the stories are destined to lead.

The streets on which the boys live are narrow and unexciting. The narrator in "Araby" lives on a "blind" (861) street in the city of Dublin. Joyce describes the street as "blind" to allow the reader to understand that the boy will never escape from the dead end life that he is currently living. Standing at the end of the "blind" street, watching over the other dull, unchanging homes is a vacant two-story house, representing a life leading to emptiness. Frank McCourt, author and narrator of *Angela's Ashes: A Memoir*, also lives on such a street. Frank lives in Limerick, a much poorer city than Dublin. Frank also lives on a dead end street, but his street does not have a vacant two-story house at its end. Instead, Frank McCourt's street ends with a lavatory, the "lavatory for the whole lane" that has never been cleaned unless "it was done by someone in the middle of the night when no one was looking'" (112).

The homes in which the narrators live are as joyless as the streets upon which they stand. Before the family in Joyce's story moved into their house, it had been unoccupied for some time. The air remains thick with dust. Littering the rooms are moldy books and papers that belonged to the former tenant, a priest. The garden behind the house grows wild and unkempt, proving that even the late priest had not cared to improve his environment. The house in which Frank McCourt and his family live is in worse condition than that of Joyce's character. Although the house has two levels, the first level is unfit for human habitation. When it rains, the first floor fills with floodwaters. Nothing stops the water from coming in under the door. "People emptying their buckets into the lavatory make it worse, and there is a sickening stink in the kitchen" (117). Since the entire family is confined to one room, there is no privacy. The family has no money; they have no heat; they have no food.

Being poor in Ireland, a young boy has only his youthful distractions, unless, as in Frank McCourt's case, at a young age he is held accountable for an entire family. The narrator in "Araby" can escape from the dull reality of his life for short periods of time. From reading the priest's moldy books, the narrator has developed quite an imagination. His aunt takes him to the market on Saturdays. While walking through the "flaring streets" of Dublin, the boy "thinks little of his future" (862–863). The narrator, instead, pretends that he is a knight in shining armor fending off villains (drunks and whores) and protecting his fair lady (the object of his affection). The bazaar, Araby, signifies to him all that is romantic and chivalric until he is disillusioned and left in anguish in the semi-darkened hall. Frank McCourt, on the other hand, cannot ever escape the reality of his circumstances. After his drunken father leaves, Frank is left to care for his mother and brothers. He is forced to quit school so that he can earn wages to support the family. Frank tries to save money so that he and his family can escape the bleakness of Limerick, but he does not make enough money to save any for their departure.

In the opening lines of his book, McCourt writes, "Worse than the ordinary miserable childhood is the miserable Irish childhood" (1). James Joyce and Frank McCourt utilize setting in their stories to illustrate to the reader just how miserable it was to grow up poor in Ireland's cities. The boy in "Araby" and the boy in *Angela's Ashes* will undoubtedly grow up to be miserable men. It is fated that these boys develop into discontented men who will never have the opportunity to change their living situations. There is no hope for them unless they can escape Ireland's gloominess.

Works Cited

Joyce, James. "Araby." *Literature for Composition: Essays, Fiction, Poetry, and Drama*. Eds. Sylvan Barnet et al. 5th ed. New York: Longman, 2000. 861–865.

McCourt, Frank. *Angela's Ashes: A Memoir*. New York: Touchstone, 1999.

Under the Tip of the Metaphor

Louis Castellano

Assignment: In this out-of-class essay, the student was to examine how two poems use metaphor to convey meaning.

Metaphors have become a simple part of life. Our speech and our thoughts work with metaphors as levers for communication and comprehension. The metaphor is also one of the best methods for catching the abstract in a communicable form. As hand motions help us explain more accurately physical details that are tedious to put into words, so do metaphors help us explain and grasp complex thoughts. In the poems "Word" and "Pitcher," by Stephen Spender and Robert Francis respectively, each author is describing what it means to be a poet. Metaphors become the ideal tools for Spender and Francis to describe themselves, and with the metaphors, their communication is clear and concise.

In "Word," Stephen Spender explains a humorous relationship he sees between words and a poet, in which the poet is a fisherman and the words are the fish. Amazingly, this metaphor becomes natural when Spender's words bring it to life. We can see a poet teasing and testing words in the sea of his or her mind. Somehow the words develop into separate beings and "bite" or volunteer to be used by the poet. We call this technique of making "words" into biting fish reification. It is a method of taking what is abstract and likening it to something more concrete, which in this case is a biting fish. The reification continues throughout the rest of the poem as

Spender asks, "Shall I throw it back free . . . Or shall I pull it in / to rhyme upon a dish?" (2, 5–6). These few lines are very effective in communicating because they do not just tell us what the author thinks, they give us a scene we can visualize and understand through seeing. In this picture, words are reified as ingredients for a poetic meal, and we understand the poet personified as a fisherman-chef, with the ability to make a savory, rhyming meal if the right word is caught. The metaphor in this poem is extremely effective in eliminating wordiness and fully conveying the ideas of the author.

As in "Word," the poem "Pitcher" likewise conveys the poet's view of himself. However, this poem works not to explain the relationship between the poet and his poetic ingredients, but rather to portray the relationship between the poet and his readers. A baseball pitcher is the metaphor for the poet, and the readers are represented as those at bat. All that Francis wishes to convey is kept within this metaphor throughout the poem. Lines one through three begin, "his aim / How not to hit the mark he seems to aim at / His passion how to avoid the obvious" (1–3). This technique of disguising the point of a poem is self-evident in this very poem. The metaphor of the pitcher throwing a deceptive curve ball is parallel to the poet tossing us his ideas not straight forward, but angled with metaphors and similes. Lines five and six continue, "The others throw to be comprehended. He / Throws to be a moment misunderstood" (5–6). The metaphor continues to expound, conveying how poems are often misread at first or "a moment misunderstood" (6). The poem concludes nicely by saying, "Not to, yet still, still to communicate" (9). This completes the picture of the poet. We know that he is not a deceiver; he just communicates in a less blatant fashion. Overall, this becomes a wonderful metaphor that relates what is familiar to the audience, pitching a baseball, to what is new and less concrete, pitching a poetic concept. In addition, the author, as in the first poem, is able to compress complex thoughts into a few short, interesting sentences.

Metaphors in both these poems are rather simple. A poet is a fisherman, and a poet is a pitcher. Yet, these correlations can be explored in numerous ways to introduce us to the patterns of a wordsmith. Time is spared as metaphoric communication is concentrated. Still, metaphors leave room for implication and expansion. Finally, through these metaphors, not only can we become acquainted with the mysterious poet, but we can also enjoy our time learning with interesting and humorous comparisons. To conclude, metaphors are far more than flowery language and ammunition for wit. Metaphors are translators, time savers, and even pleasures.

Works Cited

Francis, Robert. "Pitcher." *Text Book: Writing through Literature*. Ed. Robert Scholes, Nancy R. Comley, and Gregory L. Ulmer. 3rd ed. New York: Bedford / St. Martin's, 2002. 89–90.

Spender, Stephen. "Word." *Text Book: Writing through Literature*. Ed. Robert Scholes, Nancy R. Comley, and Gregory L. Ulmer. 3rd ed. New York: Bedford / St. Martin's, 2002. 89.

An Explication of John Donne's "The Flea"

Myredith Gonzales

Assignment: In this out-of-class essay, the student was to explicate a poem.

In John Donne's poem, "The Flea," a man attempts to seduce a woman by using the title's insect to reason that losing her virginity will be no more damaging to her than a flea bite. Donne's poem is organized into three stanzas, each containing nine lines. His use of metaphors, images, and highly ingenious reasoning presents a convincing argument for the characters' relationship.

In the first stanza, the main character speaks to his lover, and tells her to take note of the insect that has just bitten him: "Mark but this flea" (1). Donne's use of the word "but" indicates the unworthiness of the flea. The words "mark in this" calls to the attention of the flea's interior, which contains the man's blood and his lover's blood: "It sucked me first, and now sucks thee, / And in this flea our bloods mingled be;" (3–4). Here, Donne presents the image of their united blood: "It sucked me first, and now sucks thee" (3). He purposely selects the word "sucked," which has a sexual connotation and adds to the sensuality of the poem. The audience learns that this is a seduction poem; the young man is arguing that what his lover is denying him, which is her virginity, represented by her blood, is of little importance. His metaphor of a worthless flea diminishes the importance of the woman's virginity.

As the stanza continues, the main character argues that the blood contained within the flea cannot be "A sin, nor shame, nor loss of maidenhead" (6). In society and in most religions, pre-marital sex was considered shameful or a sin since it was the equivalent to a woman losing her virginity.

Donne also makes the point that the flea has successfully obtained his lover's blood without any effort: "Yet this enjoys before its woo" (7). He challenges his lover by making this point and questions her as to why the flea can savor her sweetness while he cannot; therefore, the flea is "pampered" (8). The speaker uses the word "swell" to call to mind the excitement that occurs in sexual activity. At the end of the stanza, the speaker tells his lover, "And this, alas, is more than we would do" (9). He is truly disappointed with knowing that the flea is far more privileged than he.

As the speaker continues in the second stanza, he presents his lover with two significant metaphors. He says, "Oh stay, three lives in one flea spare, / Where we almost, yea more than married are. / This flea is you and I. . ." (10–12). Here, the speaker means that their lives are within the flea and not just the flea's blood. They are the additional two lives that join the flea's life. He purposely chooses the word "spare" to once again indicate that the flea is unimportant. Since he and his lover are part of the flea, he is diminishing their importance. Although this seems strange for the speaker to imply that they are unimportant, it emphasizes his point that her virginity is meaningless. As the poem continues, the speaker views the flea as a place where they have more than a marital relationship: "Where we almost, yea more than married are" (11). Donne uses a second metaphor to stress this marriage: ". . .and this Our marriage bed, and marriage temple is;" (12–13). Here, the speaker hopes that his lover will conclude that if they can be married inside the flea, which implies that they are allowed to have sex, then in all actuality, they should have the same relationship outside of the flea.

In line 14, the speaker mentions society's general view of pre-marital sex. The "parent's grudge" represents the social idea that pre-marital sex is shameful and is considered a sin. The speaker continues and apprehensively directs his thoughts specifically to his lover: "Though parents grudge, and you. . ." (14). Donne strategically places a comma before "and you" to display this phrase as an afterthought. The placement of this comma within this line shows that the speaker is at first hesitant to acknowledge that his lover is also resistant to his advances; however, he emphasizes that "we are met" (14). He makes the point that despite the degrading thoughts of society, their blood is still combined in the flea. The idea that he and his lover are the only two people who know that their blood is mixing within the flea indicates that the speaker believes that the world may never realize that the combination of their blood is a sexual act.

In the second stanza's final tercet, he says that the act of killing this flea would be considered murder of the flea, him, and his lover: "And sacrilege, three sins in killing three" (18). If his lover follows her natural tendency to dispose the flea, the speaker argues that her act would be "sacrilege" since she would be denying and destroying a union that is so sacred.

Finally, in the last stanza, the speaker's lover kills the flea: "Cruel and sudden, hast thou since / Purpled thy nail in blood of innocence" (19–20). Here, the speaker suggests two ideas: first, the line shows that although their blood is mixed, which represents their intimate relationship, the blood is still innocent. Second, the speaker presents the idea that since his lover has shown little regard for the innocence of the flea, then why should she not do the same with her own innocence? The speaker continues to emphasize the flea's innocence by saying, "Wherein could this flea guilty be, / Except in that drop which it sucked from thee?" (21–22). These two ideas strengthen the speaker's argument and reasoning. As the speaker continues his argument, he says, "Yet thou triumph'st, and say'st that thou Find'st not theyself nor me the weaker now" (lines 23–24). The speaker implies that since the status of their relationship did not change as a result of the flea's death, the blood, therefore, was unimportant. Once again, the speaker decreases the significance of the flea to compliment his argument. In this stanza's final tercet, the speaker completely dismisses his lover's dread and apprehension towards pre-marital sex: " 'Tis true; then learn how false fears be" (25). Donne's use of the word "fears" places more responsibility on her apprehension of pre-marital sex, rather than society's views, which he previously mentions within the poem. The speaker feels that it is because of her personal fear that they are not able to consummate their relationship rather than society's disapproval of pre-marital sex.

Donne closes the poem by focusing the speaker's final argument on convincing his lover that negative consequences will not occur as a result of their physical union. To validate this argument, Donne finishes the poem by saying, "Just so much honor, when thou yield'st to me, / Will waste, as this flea's death took life from thee" (26–27). This line recalls the lover's fears that were previously mentioned. The speaker's lover is afraid that the world will find out if she agrees to the sexual act, and that she will be completely humiliated and demoted by society. The word 'waste' calls to mind that she has a fear of throwing away her honor if she disregards these concerns. However, the speaker does not pay attention to her concerns and instead, finds her apprehension foolish. In the last line, he nails his argument. The speaker proves to his lover that losing her virginity will have no more of an effect on her than the destruction of their combined blood within the flea.

Throughout the poem, Donne alternates lines of iambic tetrameter and iambic pentameter. He varies the rhythm to stress particular words and phrases and to reflect the twists that he occasionally makes in his arguments. This variation of the rhythm can be seen in lines 25–27: "'Tis true; then learn how false, fears be; / Just so much honor, when they yield'st to me, / Will waste, as this flea's death took life from thee." Here, the speaker contorts his argument to make the point that his lover will lose nothing if she gives herself to him. In the first stanza, he states, "Mark but this flea, and mark in this" (1). Here, Donne stresses the first word "Mark" instead of beginning with an unstressed syllable. Finally, Donne's poem follows the aabbccddd rhyme scheme. The consistency of this pattern mirrors the persistence that the speaker presents as he proceeds with his request for intimacy.

Throughout "The Flea," Donne manages to find arguments in the flea's living state and in its death. He ingeniously argues through verse by shifting the limits of a flea to a couple's entire world.

Works Cited

Donne, John. "The Flea." The Bedford Introduction to Literature: Reading, Thinking, Writing. 7th ed. Ed. Michael Meyer. Boston: Bedford / St. Martin's, 2005. 1200.

London and Its Falling Bridges

Jon Brinser

Assignment: In this out-of-class essay, the student was to analyze an essay from assigned selections.

William Blake's "London" cautions that industrialized civilization constricts, corrupts, and destroys lives through his use of imagery. "London" is a four stanza poem that displays different ways that civilization affects people and life. Blake's use of imagery connects with the readers and brings a sense of truth to display the theme of the poem concerning industrialized civilization. This poem highlights a chain effect that is influenced by an idea that is not normally thought of as constrictive, corruptive, and destructive by many people. Blake illustrates the foundation of our society's corruption and downfall. Step by step, constriction leads to corruption, and corruption leads to destruction.

In the first stanza, imagery is used to show how constrictiveness can affect people and life. In the first line, Blake tells how the streets are "chartered," or defined by law. The restricted street is "near where the chartered Thames does flow" (2). This line reflects the restriction of the Thames River, in which the river symbolizes purity, innocence, and new beginning. The constriction of the river indicates the constriction of new beginning, innocence, and purity. The last two lines of the first stanza describe how people are restricted, governed, and controlled physically. The constriction of the people is not only a physical constriction, but it also brings weakness and woe as a result of their misfortune. As the author writes, "in every face I meet / marks of weakness, marks of woe" (3–4). These lines describe the impact that constrictiveness has on the people's lives. It shows that they are not only physically restricted but also mentally affected.

In the second stanza, Blake illustrates how civilization is mentally and emotionally constrictive. In the fifth and sixth lines, the author makes clear that the result of civilization is reflected upon everyone of every age. Blake states "in every voice, in every ban, / the mind-forged manacles I hear" (7–8). These lines show that all people's cries come from the foundation of the confinements and restraints in their lives. This reflects that civilization constricts lives and that these constrictions have negative impacts on peoples' lives, which in turn supports the theme that industrialized civilization constricts, corrupts, and destroys lives. These minds are forged by the lack of education for people, which directly constricts the lives of many. This stanza illustrates that the prohibitions and restrictions are mentally and emotionally bearing on the people of all ages.

The poem moves from telling of how people are physically, mentally, and emotionally affected to how they are morally affected in the third stanza. The third stanza further illustrates the corruption of life as a result of industrialized civilization with the use of imagery. In the ninth and tenth lines, Blake writes "how the Chimney-sweeper's cry / every black'ning Church appalls" (9–10). These lines reflect how the industrialized civilization is corrupting the lives of chimney-sweepers. These chimney sweepers are not people working for money to rear and support families; they are orphans earning their stay at the orphanage. Children who are a symbol of purity and innocence are being forced to clean chimneys including those of the churches. Not only are the orphans' lives corrupted, but they are corrupted by corrupt institutions, which are run by corrupted men. The imagery of the "black'ning Church" illustrates the corruption stained in the church by the association of allowing abuse of orphans. This line clearly shows that industrialized civilization has corrupted even the holiest of places such as the churches. The last two lines of this stanza illustrate the constricted, corrupted, and destroyed lives of the unfortunate and helpless soldiers who are ordered to battle by the government (11–12). These are orders coming from the corrupted government, which is motivated by greed. These men are sent to surrender their lives as a result of industrialized civilization. The corruption caused by industrialized civilization is a chain which spreads throughout everyone's lives.

Blake, in the fourth stanza, illustrates the way that industrialized civilization leads to the destruction of people's lives. The last stanza reflects the most significant result of industrialized civilization. Blake tells about "how the youthful Harlot's curse / blasts the new-born Infant's tear, / and blights with plagues the Marriage hearse," which describes the chain of one's corrupted life leads the corruption and destruction of many others (15–17). He tells us about how "Harlot's curse," which is the sexually transmitted disease known as syphilis, blinds the babies of its victims. The disease spreads through families due to non-loyal men and the use of prostitutes. These men are affected by disease carrying prostitutes and go home and spread it to their wives and families. This is a cycle of corruption and destruction that is displayed by Blake through his use of the paradox "Marriage hearse" (17). This is an indirect result of the industrialized civilization which is complementary to the poem's theme.

Peoples' lives are changed for the worse due to the constrictiveness of industrialized civilization. In everyday life, people are constricted by rules and regulations. This poem shows that industrialized civilization has led to the corruption of all things, even the things that are most significant to most people such as church, family, and the government. The greed that is associated with industrial civilization is the factor that leads to the corruption of all things. This poem depicts a theme that is not only true in this poem, but also in everyday life. It illustrates the theme that industrialized civilization constricts, corrupts, and destroys lives.

Works Cited

Blake, William. "London." *Literature and its Writers: A Compact Introduction to Fiction, Poetry, and Drama.* Ed. Ann And Samuel Charters. 3rd ed. Boston: Bedford, 2004. 845.

Evolution of Trane

James Larimer

Assignment: In this out-of-class assignment, the student was to select a poem or pair of poems and develop an analysis that exhibits one of the critical formats discussed in class.

Amiri Baraka's poem entitled "AM/TRAK," is a stunning exposé on the musical life of John Williams Coltrane (Trane). Baraka skillfully highlights the musical career of one of the most prolific jazz saxophonists and composers in history. "AM/TRAK" parallels African Americans social unrest of the late 1960's with the emotional fervor of Trane's artistry. Through a first person limited perspective, Baraka skillfully binds his poem on the themes of history, love, and the word "scream." The first stanza sets up and introduces a three part outline on this theme: "History Love Scream Oh" (602).

Baraka's undeniable knowledge of Trane's life and career is impressively highlighted in near perfect chronology, thus, beginning the poem with Trane's history. As a noted jazz critic, Baraka's book entitled *Black Music* supports the historical connotations interjected throughout "AM/TRAK." In lines 15–16, the speaker purposely refers to three influential jazz musicians in Trane's formidable years. Cleanhead (Eddie Vinson), Diz (Dizzy Gillespie) and Big Maybelle (Maybelle Carter) are mentors who personally shaped Trane's musical career. The metaphor on line 16, "Trees in the shining night forest," signifies a reverence for these famous musicians. As Trane's career is highly chronicled, Alyn Shipton's, *A New History of Jazz* notes that from 1946–1951, Trane performed with Cleanhead, Diz, and Big

Maybelle in Philly (741). Such musical giants were instrumental in equipping Trane for the next level of challenge.

The transition before the third stanza, "Honk Oh scream— Miles comes," leads readers to 1955 when Trane started performing in Miles Davis's band. This was his first stage of serious notoriety (Shipton 744). Although joining Miles allowed Trane to become a household name in the jazz world, verse three describes the relatively sedate "cool jazz" period in Miles's band; thus, garnering Trane from stretching the limits of his technical and harmonic virtuosity. The speaker makes the following observations:

> Miles wd stand back and negative check
> oh, he dug him—Trane
> But Trane clawed at the limits of cool
> Slandered sanity
> With his tryin to be born
> Raging
> Shit. (46–52)

This clearly describes Trane's artistic frustration by the restrictiveness of cool jazz, not to mention, working under the reportedly difficult leadership of Miles Davis. Baraka's statement, "Before the trilogy, and after, say, the Columbia album with Miles Davis, *Milestones*, it became increasingly evident to anyone who would listen that Coltrane was definitely moving into fresher areas of expression on his instrument," explains Trane's yearning to push the traditional boundaries of music (Jones 58).

Another milestone of Trane's career is highlighted in the fourth stanza. The speaker notes, "There was nothing left to do but be where monk cd find him" (70) implying that Trane was yearning to take his music to another level. As Thelonious Monk (Monk) was noted as one of the compositional genuses of his time, Trane entered higher education by way of another musical legend. Master T (Thelonious Monk), Shadow (Shadow Wilson), and Wilbur (Wilbur Ware), noted in lines 106–110, comprised the members of Monk's exclusive, ground breaking, quartet in 1957. Baraka notes, "Monk, it seemed, opened Trane's head to possibilities of rhythmic and harmonic variation that Trane had never considered before," once again alluding to Trane's continual musical growth (Jones 60). Last but not least was Trane's own band, as described in the following lines:

> The cadre came together
> The inimitable 4 who blew the pulse of then, exact

The flame the confusion the love of
Whatever the fuck there was
To love (142–145)

By no coincidence, the speaker lists each member of this final revolutionary band: "Jimmy Garrison, bass, McCoy Tyner, piano, Captain Marvel Elvin on drums" (171). Shipton states, "This flexible and sympathetic group of colleagues accompanied Coltrane's rise to cult status in the early 1960s, and was crucial in creating the body of work through which he subsequently had most influence on the course of jazz" (754). Offering further testimony, Baraka states, "the rest of the group, especially Elvin Jones (Captain Marvel Elvin) can scare you to death" proving the emotional power and influence of Trane's ultimate complement of musicians (Jones 67).

Moving on to the second part of the outline focuses on Baraka's use of the word love. The speaker's comments describe Trane's multidimensional expressions of love, poured out through his saxophone:

Honk Honk Honk, "I am hear
To love
It." Let me be fire-mystery
Air feeder beauty" (30–33)

Ironically, having been accused of being one of the most aggressive and technical saxophonists, his ability to play a beautiful love ballad was arguably second to none. Referring to such ability as described by A.B. Spellman on the liner notes from *John Coltrane and Johnny Hartman*, "[Trane] plays a solo that is at once relaxing, poignant, strong, romantic, danceable, complex and beautiful" (qtd. In Coltrane 8). The repeated use of the word "love" could also signify Trane's spiritual awakening after being fired by Miles Davis for drug use. Leonard Brown's biography of John Coltrane quotes Trane as follows: "I experienced, by the grace of God, a spiritual awakening which was to lead me to a richer, fuller, more productive life, in gratitude; I humbly asked to be given the means and privilege to make others happy through music." Brown further writes, "In 1964, John recorded the album, "A Love Supreme" which was very spiritually oriented. His music became increasingly religious in nature, focusing on spiritual concepts of life from Africa and Asia as well as western Christianity." Baraka's emphasis on "love" could very well point to the transformation of Trane's life during this period; in addition, *A Love Supreme* was one of Trane's biggest selling recordings.

Finally, the word "scream" sets up Trane's feelings of oppression from the social injustices of the times. Baraka's repeated usage of onomatopoeia as in line 148, "blow, oh honk-scram (bahhhhhhh — wheeeeeee), symbolizes Trane's social protest through music. Shipton's description of Trane's sound shows a similarity to the poem's use of onomatopoeia: "He created a distinctive raw tone on tenor . . . including vocal tones, multiphonics, honks, squeals, and high, shrieking harmonics" (740). The speaker's voice throughout "AM/TRAK" employs a stream-of-consciousness closely related to the improvisational language employed in Trane's solos. As sure as Trane's music is highlighted, Baraka's own tone of aggressive anger permeates "AM/TRAK." Within each progressive stanza of Trane's musical career lies a more intense scream of outrage. Considering "AM/TRAK" was written during the tumultuous 1960's, it is easy to identify the cause for such emotional outrage. The author's intent on correlating Trane's music with the turbulence of the times is evident:

> Trane was the spirit of the 60's
> He was Malcom X in New Super Bop Fire
> Baaahhhh . . . (154–155)

Ironically, considering Trane's revolutionary style, he continued to draw creativity from a clear focus on religious and spiritual messages until his death in 1967. Writing compositions such as "Prayer and Affirmation," "Meditations," "Compassion," and "Dear Lord," he lit the path for others to follow.

A close analysis of Amiri Baraka's "AM/TRAK" passionately chronicles the musical genius of one of America's greatest jazz musicians; in addition, Baraka candidly captures the mindset of being African American in the 1960's.

Works Cited

Baraka, Amiri. "AM/TRAK." Schakel & Ridl. 602–607.

Brown, Leonard. "John Coltrane Biography." 2005. 23 Mar. 2005. <http://www.jcmc.neu.edu/jcbio.html>

Coltrane, John. *John Coltrane and Johnny Hartman*. Impulse GRD-157, 1995.

Jones, Leroi. *Black Music*. New York: Da Capo Press, 1968. 58–68.

Schakel, Peter and Jack Ridl, eds. *Approaching Literature in the 21st Century*. Boston: Bedford/St. Martin's, 2005.

Shipton, Alyn. *A New History of Jazz*. New York: Continuum, 2002. 740–754.

Dual Selves in
Sylvia Plath's "Elm"

Meghan Pye

Assignment: In this researched essay written out of class, the student was to analyze a poem by an assigned author.

Since her final and fatal suicide attempt in the winter of 1963, American poet Sylvia Plath has garnered literary recognition and cult figure status. Despite her deteriorating mental and emotional health, she churned out an entire collection of poems during her last three months, the posthumous publication *Ariel*. As in the poem "The Moon and the Yew Tree," Plath writes about a tree that stood beside her home in Devon, England. The poem "Elm" was considered a crucial stylistic development, marking the beginning of her late poetry and its break from transitional poetry (Rosenblatt 87). Through utilizing a duality of self as both a human being and a natural object, Plath illustrates her inner torment and longing for release in "Elm."

"Elm" has fourteen stanzas consisting of three lines each. Written in free verse, the poem is structured around an extended metaphor embodied by the elm tree. "[Sylvia Plath] is not prodigal in her use of metaphor—only one to a poem usually. She establishes her metaphor and then moves it about . . . until it defines precisely the statement she wishes to make" (Stubblefield 270). Appearing originally in *The New Yorker* as "The Elm Speaks," the poem's title is indicative of its being a dramatic monologue (Wu 648). Though Rosenblatt claims that the speaker is the elm tree (153), Wu points out that the poet's "use of three pronouns—"she," "I," and "you"— can be read as the divided selves of one identity as well as three separate roles" (648).

The poem begins with the self-identity listening to the elm tree, who seems to be painfully aware of the poet's fears: "I know the bottom, she says. I know it with my great tap root [sic]. It is what you fear. I do not fear it: I have been there" (Plath 1–3). The tree seems to be not a foreign object, but rather an externalization of self through which she is thinking (Rosenblatt 154). In this first stanza, Holbrook seems to feel that Plath "has been taught debasement and brought down to the bottom . . . among lesser creatures" (53). On the contrary, her roots seem to deal less with shame and more with the frightful knowledge found in the depths of the earth, the core of the soul.

The sea churns out its steady voice of dissatisfactions. The murmur of discontent, the sound of nothing, is enough to fill or consume the poet's thoughts to the point of madness. The elm continues, admitting the intangibility of love and the ensuing, emptying effect. "Love is a shadow. How you lie and cry after it" (Plath 7–8). With the sound of hooves as heartbeats, off it gallops into the night, leaving only a faint echo. Then comes the question "Or shall I bring you the sound of poisons? This is rain now, this big hush" (Plath 13–14). The rain, like love, bears no wholesome fruit, only that which is "tin-white, like arsenic" (Plath 15).

Nature and human assume interchangeable roles in stanzas six through nine. Sunsets suffered daily have scorched her precious filaments—the sustenance of the tree, the optical nerves of the woman. Wu relates this to the "loss of love ('sunsets'), [by which] her lifeblood ('red filaments') is reduced to broken nerves ('a hand of wires')" (648). Burning like an uncontrollable love, the sun has rendered the fibrous strands useless. The inner torment of the mind is comparable to the storm that the elm must weather. "The self in despair becomes a bundle of weapons ('I fly about like clubs')" (Holbrook 7). Such splitting and fragmenting images are congruent with the schizophrenic's descent into madness (Holbrook 127). Even as the storm subsides, the moon offers no solace: she is "merciless: she would drag me / Cruelly, being barren" (Plath 22–23). Barren, she creates no light; she merely reflects the truth of the harsh sun. When

Plath lets go of the moon, it is "diminished and flat," (Plath 26). The menacing bulge of the nighttime moon fades into a powdery disc, yet still its "bad dreams possess and endow [her]" (Plath 27).

Perhaps worse than the nightmares is the inner cry, the longing for love and the fear of love. "Nightly it flaps out / Looking, with its hooks, for something to love" (Plath 29–30).

Works Cited

Holbrook, David. *Sylvia Plath: Poetry and Existence*. London: Athlone Press, 1976.

Melander, Ingrid. *The Poetry of Sylvia Plath: A Study of Themes*. Stockholm: Almqvist and Wiksell, 1972.

Riley, Carolyn, ed. "Sylvia Plath." *Contemporary Literary Criticism*. 140 vols. Detroit: Gale Research Company, 1973.

Rosenblatt, Jon. *Sylvia Plath: The Poetry of Initiation*. Chapel Hill: University of North Carolina Press, 1979.

Wu, Qingyun. "Elm." *Masterplots II Poetry Series*. Ed. Frank N. Magil. 9 vols. Pasadena: Salem Press, Inc., 1992.

The Darkness of Light

Kimberly McClung

*Assignment: In this out-of-class essay, the student
was asked to analyze how poets use imagery to
communicate.*

In William Stafford's poem, "Traveling through the Dark,"
our many senses are flooded with images throughout the poem.
During our class discussion on imagery and its uses we defined
imagery as anything to do with or appealing to the senses. Stafford
appeals to the senses of sight and sound in an extremely sophisti-
cated way in his poem. The images of light and dark and sound and
silence create not only a visual and auditory image but also an overall impression of the eternal conflict between man and nature.

The sense of sight is very instrumental in both a literal and a
symbolic way in this poem. The narrator, the driver of the car, is
driving down a country road in complete darkness. As the road
curves, he spots a deer lying in the road, and he stops the car to
remove the deer, knowing the deer is a great safety hazard. His matter of fact tone and his casual demeanor tell the reader that this driver is accustomed to these types of situations. He travels dark roads
often, and is aware of the danger those deer present. He knows
exactly what to do, telling us that, "it is usually best to roll them
into the canyon" (line 3). However, when he pulls past the deer and
goes back to remove it from the road, he notices that the doe is very
near giving birth. The only light by which he sees this is the "glow
of the tail-light" (line 5). Any country driver knows that tail lights

are not very bright, especially when trying to pierce through the otherwise complete darkness. And when the driver realizes the fawn is still alive, he hesitates, still in complete darkness, trying to decide what to do. The only literal light by which he comes to his decision is the dim tail light. And symbolically, he comes to his decision in dim light as well. The only light he has is his knowledge of what is the best thing to do in this situation, the logical thing to do, and that is to roll the deer into the river. He hesitates because he knows by doing that he will be causing darkness and death to come to the fawn. As he ponders the best action to take, he says he "stood in the glare off the warm exhaust turning red" (line 15). The mental picture is very vivid here, that of a dead doe with a man standing over her, visible to our mind's eye by only a cloudy red light. The haze of the light is like the confusion, the hesitation of the moment. And the rising red exhaust reminds us of blood and death, of a fatal decision made in the half light. All the images of brightness and darkness, of dim color and of broken light bring the decision in this poem to life. We do not simply see a dimly lit mountain road; we see the dying doe and her helpless fawn. We do not simply see the glow of tail lights; we see the callousness of man. And reflected in the changing light we glimpse the conflict between nature and man at the heart of this poem.

During our class discussion of this poem, we mentioned only briefly the sense of sound unveiled in this piece. However, the sounds and the silence in this poem unveil its meaning as well. The mountain road was surely silent, save the sounds of sleeping nature when the man's car happened along. He stops the car, and the only sounds we hear are coming from the car, where "under the hood purred the steady engine" (line 14). The only sounds here are man's sounds of disturbance, not nature's sounds of comfort. Nature is quiet, waiting to hear the driver's decision. "Around our group I could hear the wilderness listen" (line 16). The wilderness is listening patiently, waiting for the man to either roll the deer into the canyon or save the fawn. Logic eventually wins out in the man's mind, but not before a long moment of thought—a silent meditation of the coming decision and a seeming reverence for nature's loss. In this moment of unified silence, nature and the man seem to come to the same conclusion: saving the fawn's life is fruitless. Yet, all pause for a moment of reflection, a silent pause when all come to understand the significance of these events which have taken place this silent evening. The significance of many events such as this one lies in its reactions. The horror of many events, of which this is one, comes when the event begins to become a casual, everyday occurrence. The tragedy of events is that we can speak of them calmly, as the man spoke at first of this loss of life. What he is doing in this moment, however, is realizing the danger of apathy. The man is seeing that in the great realm of life, he is just that, a man, but he represents all men. And this doe and her fawn represent all of nature. And when he realizes these things, with nature listening in, he says he "thought hard for us all" (line 17). He thinks of the casual manner in which so many regard death, particularly that of animals. He thinks of the disregard so many of his fellow men have for death and for life as well. Nature knows it has lost a doe and her fawn, but in this incident it has regained a man—a man who, when he comes face to face with nature and man's negative impact on it, comes away with a profound reverence for nature and for life.

The visual and the auditory images we receive in this poem give us a literal picture of the event. We see a man and a deer in the dark silence, but we also see more than that. We see nature's silent reverence, man's impending darkness, and the decision's dark and silent implications. Light, noise, darkness, silence—all of these images give us one powerful overall impression of this event. This is an image of man's loud interruptions into nature's reverent silence, and of nature's peaceful darkness in contrast to man's intrusive light.

Works Cited

Stafford, William. "Traveling through the Dark." *Responding to Literature.* Ed. Judith A. Stanford. Mountain View, CA: Mayfield Publishing Company, 1999. 1150.

The Strike of Death

Tamie Lavelle Meeks

Assignment: In this out-of-class paper, the student was to explore the use of figurative language in a poem.

The major turning points in life, such as love, marriage, and death, are sometimes the hardest circumstances to describe accurately. As a result, many people tend to describe the situations more clearly by using figurative language. In Ruth Whitman's poem, "Castoff Skin," several images help to describe the speaker's experience with the death of her grandmother. In the class discussion of "Castoff Skin," we explored the images of the grandmother and came to see her as one who was once full of life but is now very thin and fragile, but we failed to discuss the speaker's attitude toward the images of her grandmother. The images incorporated into the poem show how the grandmother is affected by death, but they also express the speaker's uneasiness toward the idea of death.

At the beginning of the poem, the speaker acknowledges her grandmother's loss of vitality. When the grandmother is on her death bed, the speaker recalls the grandmother saying, "*Pretty good figure / for an old lady . . .*" (Whitman 1168). By this statement, the reader can conclude that the old lady said these words only a few years earlier. At the time of the grandmother's utterance, she was a lively and spirited old lady. She was not in her mid twenties or thirties but was probably in her eighties, yet she still claimed to have a good figure. She is not arrogant; rather, she is full of life. As the speaker remembers the vitality of her grandmother, the old lady is "l[ying] in her girlish sleep at ninety-six" (1168). This image is strange because the woman is ninety-six years old but is being described as "girlish." As suggested in class, the "girlish sleep" could describe the position in which the old woman is sleeping. She could be curled up in the fetal position. The image that is projected, though, is of a young girl still in the fragile state of growing. In reference to the grandmother, the phrase suggests the old lady's second childhood. Rather than having the independence she was used to, the old lady is now dependent on others. Just as young children need to be looked after, old people need the same kind of care as they become unable to provide for themselves. Because of this image, the speaker begins to fear death. She is seeing how death can change a lively old woman into an inactive old lady. While the image of the young girl in her peaceful sleep appears to be comforting, the image is actually unsettling for the speaker because it implies a loss of life for the elderly.

Not only does the speaker remark on the loss of her grandmother's liveliness, but she also describes the fragility of her grandmother. The speaker pictures the old lady as "small as a twig" (1168). While this simile could possibly support the curled-up position in which the grandmother is sleeping, it more accurately suggests the frailty of the woman. A twig is perceived as a small, frail piece of a tree or branch that is easily broken. The woman, if pictured as a twig, is now seen to be very thin and easily breakable. The speaker further emphasizes the feebleness of her grandmother near the end of the poem. As the speaker kisses her grandmother good bye, possibly at the funeral, she claims to kiss a "paper cheek" (1168). Because paper is thin, pale, and often weak, the paper cheek provides the image of a thin and pale old woman. Like a twig, paper can also be torn easily. Both of these images reflect the frailty and lifeless picture of the grandmother that the speaker finds troubling. While the grandmother used to be colorful and strong, she now appears to be colorless and weak.

Because the transformation from a vibrant, active woman to a dull, weak old lady is so sudden, the speaker uses a metaphor of a snake to describe the grandmother's appearance as well as to depict life and death. The speaker sees her grandmother as "leaving a tiny stretched transparence / behind her" (1168). The "transparence" is a metaphor for a snake's skin. A snake sheds his skin, leaving it behind as a sign of life; yet the skin itself is lifeless. While the skin is still apparent, there is no trace of the life that occupied the skin. Just as the snake moves onto another life, the old lady is also preparing to move onto another life in heaven. The speaker, though, is left only with a lifeless image of her grandmother "crawl[ing] away" (1168). This idea suggests a slow process by which the woman is "leaving a tiny stretched transparence / behind her" (1168). She is slowly losing the vitality that was so visible a few years earlier. The transition from her lively nature to her fragile nature is gradual. The metaphor of the snake is also used to explain death. This metaphor begins when the speaker kisses her grandmother's cheek and "[thinks] of the snake, / of his quick motion" (1168). The quickness that the speaker is referring to is the snake's strike. While a snake may crawl along the ground slowly, its strike is fast and often deadly. For the speaker, her grandmother's death was unexpected and came quickly. Now that the speaker has seen how quickly death takes life, leaving only a "transparent" reminder behind, she becomes frightened and disquieted by the idea of death.

By using figurative language, the author allows the reader to view the speaker and the grandmother in a way that can be easily pictured. The imagery also allows the reader to see the speaker's attitude toward death. Not only does the metaphor of the snake suggest the quickness of death, but it also provides the speaker with an uneasiness toward death. While the images of the snake help to provide a troubling view of death, the snake alone seems to suggest something sinister about death. It shows the unpleasant, negative side of death. Just as a snake symbolizes evil and ugliness, death is portrayed as unloving and frightful. The speaker, knowing how quickly death can come, is afraid of death. She has seen a lively, independent grandmother become a delicate, dependent old lady in a relatively short period of time. Although some of the images, such as "girlish sleep," seem to suggest a peaceful death, all of the images support the central metaphor of the snake providing a troubled, frightening view of death.

Works Cited

Whitman, Ruth. "Castoff Skin." *Responding to Literature*. Ed. Judith A. Stanford. Mountain View, CA: Mayfield Publishing Company, 1992. 1167–1168.

Walking Tall

Shalonda Jackson

Assignment: In this out-of-class essay of 600 words, the student was to compare and/or contrast two poems.

"Mr. Z" by M. Carl Holman is disappointing and negative at its best. It does a wonderful job of illustrating how the potential for truth can drive an individual into the farthest depths of ignorance and denial. On the other hand, "Still I Rise" by Maya Angelou offers inspiration and courage to anyone who reads the message contained within its lines. It is clearly evident that the speakers are different and are expressing different opinions on their ethnicity. The speaker in "Mr. Z" resembles a male in his thirties who has not grown spiritually through adversity. He thrives on ignorance and "dissension," living in fear that one day his past will catch up with him. In contrast, the speaker in "Still I Rise" suggests a female in her late teens or early twenties who is comfortable with her birthright and what it has to grant her spiritually. It appears as though she is gaining energy and strength from her conquered adversaries who wish to keep her in a state of oppression. "Mr. Z" and "Still I Rise" utilize differences in time, diction, and title selection to convey strongly opposing viewpoints to the perception of black identity.

The idea of a specific time frame is important when addressing each of these poems. In "Mr. Z" the lingering and tarnished effects of slavery were branded into the psyche of the speaker at an early age. From the time "Mr. Z" was "taught that his mother's skin was a sign of error" (1), he carried around excess baggage that being black was a sign of inferiority. He assimilated "whatever ground was Anglo-Saxonized" (8) as a method of rejecting all that was his ancestry. In opposition to the viewpoint of "Mr. Z," the speaker in "Still I Rise" projects a message that has an ageless essence. There is a true sense of timelessness due to the nature of the speaker's message, which could be applied to African-Americans, all minorities, an individual person, and even women in general. There will always be a point in time in which some form of humanity is being oppressed. Even though the persona in "Still I Rise" quotes ancestral roots, she does not cast off all past affiliations with her culture. In contrast, the speaker not only accepts these situations as true links to herself, but also latches onto them with the strength of steel vices. In this particular instance, the past is not a sentence of subservient and second class citizenship, but a call to fortify the spirit with courage and resilience.

Not only is the reference to time important, but the speaker's choice of diction also allows much insight into the heart of each situation. The diction in "Mr. Z" brings with it negative connotation. At a constant and consistent rate, the speaker utilizes such words as "disclaimed" (4), "dissension" (6), "profane" (10), and "shunned" (18), when expressing personal viewpoints about the links to his heritage. It is as though "Mr. Z" is running a marathon race in order to escape everything that he is. It is ironic that while "Mr. Z" is spending most of his time turning from his "roots" (20), the speaker in "Still I Rise" is racing toward her history in order to embrace "the gifts that" her "ancestors gave" (39). She feels that she is the hope and dream of the slave. The speaker is going to use this oasis of energy to face the hostility and strife that she will endure in combat.

Perhaps the most important element in both literary works is the title, which offers the most insight into the possible nature of the poem. The title "Mr. Z" gives the impression that the speaker is nameless or that he is trying to shed the name he was born with. The single letter of the alphabet denotes a sense of anonymity and invisibility from his scarred past. In addition to the title of the poem being a single letter, it is also the last letter of the alphabet. The fact that the letter "z" is the last letter in a series of letters implies that "Mr. Z" could not get any farther from the truth. The letter "z" is the absolute end of a continuum, thereby giving influence that

"Mr. Z" went to the extreme to get away from his defective past. He has adopted and assimilated a culture that has absolutely no reference to himself while simultaneously neglecting to incorporate something of his own personal significance. On the opposite side of the spectrum is the speaker of "Still I Rise." The title of the poem, in a sense, speaks for itself. The words "Still I Rise" are a direct reflection of the poem's message and can even be found repeated many times within the context of the poem. Alone, the title is enough to encourage a showdown against adversity. The word "still" has a constancy that conjures up motivation and drive. The word "I" imbues a feeling of independence because it stands alone. Lastly, there is an encouraging pursuit to keep "rising" through all smoke-filled skies. The speaker's literally being able to elevate into the sky becomes a very important theme reflecting the determination to burst out of societal restraints. With all of these words and meanings combined, the title, standing alone, supplies the essence of what the speaker has been trying to illustrate all along.

People have many different reactions to the problems that arise in their lives and to the demons that resurface from the past. Analysis of both of these works makes it apparent that negative situations need not stay negative. Unfortunately in the case of "Mr. Z," he was a coward, a fault that denied him a true glance into who he was before he died. It is then possible for critics to debate whether the speaker really lived or not. Of course he died, but in order truly to live and be wholeheartedly spiritual, one must accept all aspects of his humanity. The speaker in "Still I Rise" vividly and boldly calls the reader to attention, requiring that the past be embraced and used as a stepping stone to freedom.

Works Cited

Angelou, Maya. "Still I Rise." *The Resourceful Writer*. Ed. William H. Bainwell. Boston: Houghton, 1987.

Holman, M. Carlos. "Mr. Z." *The Bedford Introduction to Literature*. Ed. Michael Meyer. 4th ed. Boston: Bedford - St. Martin's, 1966. 963–964.

Where There's Smoke

Diane Forrester

*Assignment: In this out-of-class essay, the student
was to write an analysis of figurative language in
a poem.*

Through class discussion of "Nighttime Fires" by Regina
Barreca, we discovered a family whose only moments of intimacy
with their father occurred at the expense of another family's destruction by fire. If we examine closely the poem's use of metaphor and
symbolism, we will see that the destructive fires this family embraced
as opportunities for bonding also represent the flames of self-
destruction that will eventually consume their father.

The title of the poem is symbolic of an emotional darkness in
which the speaker's father is enveloped by flames of hopelessness,
frustration, and hatred. Immediately into the poem we are introduced to the speaker, one of seven children, who recalls "when [she]
was five in Louisville" (1), how their father who had "lost his job"
(5), stayed up "past midnight . . . read[ing] old newspapers / with no
news" (6–7), and worked on "crosswords until he split the pencil /
between his teeth, mad" (7–8). The crossword puzzle in the paper
symbolizes the father's puzzle of providing for his family of nine
now that he is without a job and with no clue as to where the answer
can be found. These images serve to fuel the smoldering fires of
helplessness and frustration the father must feel when pondering
his jobless state and confronted by the faces of his seven children,
who depend upon him for shelter, clothing, and food.

Next we hear the "wolf whine of the siren" (9), which beckons the father and his children to the site of the fire. This use of metaphor can be interpreted as the predator's call to join the pack that is closing in on their prey, soon to feast upon the burnt carcass of another's destruction. It is the literal destruction by fire that ignites the symbolic flames of hatred and a desire for revenge that lie within the father's soul. The father's "dry, brittle heart" (18) speaks of an extremely parched, withered spiritual being, one without hope. This image gives the impression of a soul so dry and fragile that not only would it disintegrate if touched, but it is also likely to burst into flame by mere exposure to the heat of his internal fire.

The sight of huge fires, popping, cracking, and exploding "burnt wood / and a smell of flames high into the pines" (10–11) excites the father, whose "face lit up in the heat given off by destruction/like something was being set right" (19–20). It is undoubtedly the internal flames of revenge for what he perceives as his ruined financial state that result in the glow of satisfaction noted by his daughter.

While the speaker's father excitedly explores the ruin after the fire has been brought under control, our attention is drawn to the family's mother, whose eyes follow their father rather than watching the house burn. We are told that the mother isn't happy until they "were ready to go, when it is finally over/and nothing else could burn" (27–28). She too witnesses the fires of destruction raging within her husband and watches closely until she is confident that his internal fires are under control.

It is in the final two lines of the poem that the most powerful image is delivered: "I could see his quiet face in the/rearview mirror, eyes like hallways filled with smoke" (30–31). It is the only reference in the poem that acknowledges the family's awareness of the emotional fires that intermittently smolder, then rage with the father. We are given a vivid comparison of a man to a house whose hallways are filled with smoke, bestowing upon us the realization that a terrible, raging, destructive force is about to explode and consume this five-year-old child's father. Perhaps even more terrible is the knowledge that his family must stand by and watch the fires of self-destruction burn, helpless to fight them and certain that there will be little, if anything, left to salvage.

Throughout the poem, "Nighttime Fires," the uses of symbolism and metaphor combine with the vivid imagery to reveal to the reader the destructive forces at work within the speaker's father. The central symbol of the poem is fire used as a traditional symbol of destruction to reveal the powerful forces at work within the father. It is apparent to the speaker's family that the destructive emotions of hate, hopelessness, and frustration are raging within the father, just as the houses they watch are consumed by the destructive force of a raging fire. Conceivably even more frightening are the resultant embers of devastation that threaten to spark and ignite these same fires within his children, who may grow up viewing their world through "eyes like hallways filled with smoke" (31).

Works Cited

Barreca, Regina. "Nighttime Fires." *The Bedford Introduction to Literature.* Ed. Michael Meyer. 2nd ed. New York: Bedford—St. Martin's Press, 1990. 507.

The Imagery in "Love Poem"

Kryss Downs

Assignment: In this out-of-class essay, the student was to analyze the ways in which the poem's imagery communicates its theme.

"Love Poem" by John Frederick Nims may never appear on a Hallmark card, but it is a poem to be treasured by anyone who has ever known the joy of love in a lasting, ongoing relationship. The imagery of this poem carries the reader through an experience of love at its best, but also at is most real. This woman in Nims' poem may not "walk in beauty like the night," but she makes those around her smile. The love of these two people seems full of fun and passion. Like converging streams, two lines of imagery, one describing her flaws and the other describing her talents, run happily through this poem; where these streams of imagery meet, the reader is treated to a delightful torrent of joy, laughter, and love.

What begins as an eye-brow-raising image of an ultimate klutz gradually expands into an affectionate picture of joy-filled love, but not immediately. The strange salutation begins, "My clumsiest dear" (1). As readers, we double-check the title to make sure we read it right. The next four lines introduce us to a Lucy Ricardo, a portrayal almost slap-stick. "Whose hands shipwreck vases," "bulls in china," "burs in linen" are outrageous images of domestic disaster (1, 4). We visualize the glass shards across the floor and hear the china clinking and crashing. We see that even the linen closet is not safe from the hands as rough as "burs."

It is here that Nims first contrasts this stream of imagery with a new stream which paints a picture of a most generous and compassionate person. A video of desperate people plays before our eyes in the word portraits of "ill-at-ease fidgeting people," "refugee uncertain at the door" (5–6), and "drunk clambering on his undulant floor" (8). We see her taking these people in, making them comfortable, "deftly" steadying the weaving drunk. The choice of the word "deftly" springs out in contrast to the clumsiness pictured in the first four lines. His portrayal is so endearing that we admire her too. We wish we could meet her!

We return to the other stream of imagery with an account of more of her flaws. Only now we begin to see that these are really not flaws but, instead, the flesh and bones that make this picture of virtue come to life. The humor of the images becomes even broader than before. We cannot suppress a laugh at the thought of this woman waiting patiently to cross the street between cars two blocks away, yet absent-mindedly "leaping before red apoplectic streetcars" (11). Even the word "apoplectic" sounds funny when we say it as it conjures up visions of a fat man with a red face, eyes bulging. A streetcar in this condition is hilarious. The exaggerations seem designed not to hurt her feelings but to make her smile and even laugh. He says that she is not only "a wrench in clocks" but also in "the solar system" (13). We visualize a tool in awkward hands dismantling the inner workings of a fine clock, then proceeding into the stratosphere to knock out a few stars and clip the moon. But, in setting the solar system on its ear, perhaps the poet is telling his darling something about her effect on his universe. This woman's love has turned the sun, moon, and stars cockeyed and flipped his world upside down.

Once again the poet moves back to the praise of his love. He restates how she moves "at ease" with people, with words, and with love. Fourteen lines into this love poem, the author finally uses the word "love," though waiting so long to say it makes it mean more. In a play upon his earlier image of her as a "taxi driver's terror" (9), he praises her ability to "expertly maneuver" in the "traffic of wit" (16). We picture a car carefully pulling in and out of busy traffic, deftly making its way past potential trouble. We picture a gathering of friends and acquaintances tossing witty barbs about and our lady moving between egos and personalities, keeping the peace, easing in and out between hurting people. All who know her sit at her feet "all devotion" (6), like happy children around their mother.

At last the two streams of imagery rush together. We see that even the images of her clumsiness connote this couple's intimacy and closeness in "coffee spreading on our flannel" (17) and "lipstick grinning on our coat" (18). Coffee in flannel spins images of shared mornings over coffee (soon spilt by his darling, of course). The lipstick on the coat can only mean warm hugs and smiles, perhaps as he leaves for work or maybe as he returns. Then the image lifts away to a kind of abandon. What kind of passion is this that can mix images of unbreakable heaven and floating on spilt bourbon? The words seem full of memories we can only guess at, but we sense that it is the best of passion which is mixed with a little laughter and craziness.

Then, like still waters after raging rapids, the imagery of the final lines brings the reader to a dead stop. The reader is stunned by the image of the hands which have shipwrecked vases, chipped glasses, wrecked the solar system, and steadied the drunk now dropping "white and empty" (23). We see those rough, loving hands hanging limply off the side of a bed, the life gone out of them. We understand the extent her presence fills his life. The image of the toys of the world breaking at her death takes his loss to a global level. It is as though children would stop playing; fun and joy would die with her.

The imagery which at first seems strange for a love poem ends up giving a rich, multifaceted picture of true love as it happens in real life. Instead of relying on cliches, Nims has taken a variety of unexpected images and put them together for a charming, funny, touching tribute to real love.

Works Cited

Nims, John Frederick. "Love Poem." *The Bedford Introduction to Literature.* Ed. Michael Meyer. 2nd ed. New York: Bedford—St. Martin's Press. 1990. 512.

In Dependence Day

Anne M. Van Dalinda

Assignment: In this out-of-class essay, the student was to select a poem from a given list and write an explication.

At first reading, "The Fourth of July" by Howard Nemerov appears to be a poem of thanks and celebration for the freedoms enjoyed by the citizens of this country. But a closer look reveals that the fireworks display is a symbol of our basic rights. The poet uses the narrator to illustrate that government intervention in our lives is eroding the principles of freedom on which this country was founded.

On Independence Night the speaker is drunk. He could have been drinking to celebrate the holiday, or, conversely, perhaps he got drunk because he sees no reason to celebrate. As a result of his in-ebriated condition he distances himself from everyone else in both body and spirit and watches the local fireworks display "from far away" (2). From his perch on a "high hill" (3), his perspective melancholy and far-reaching, he is able to see the "stately illuminations" (5). The word "stately" is used here to emphasize not only the beauty of the magnificent fireworks but also the fact that the display is an official, regulated affair. "One light shattering in a hundred lights" (6) is not only imagery to describe a breathtaking show in the sky but is also a metaphor for the shattering of the ideal of liberty.

Gazing across "the moony green/of lakes" (3–4), the narrator drunkenly reflects on other times. He cries not just because he is "country drunk" (8) but because he longs for the simple life of his boyhood. He remembers being "allowed to buy" (11) "sparklers, rockets, roman candles" (10) and being able to create his own independent display. Although he acknowledges that this was "at some peril to life and property" (13), he appreciates the freedom to decide for himself what risks he wants to take and does not want every aspect of his life legislated by the authorities. He notes with some bemusement that "our freedom to abuse our freedom has since . . . been remedied/by legislation" (15–16).

The besotted speaker comments with wry appreciation on the "perfectly safe public display" (17) that he is now able to watch "at a distance" (18). No longer is he free to enjoy the moment of lighting and watching his own paltry show. Instead, thanks to "the contribution of all the taxpayers/together" (19–20), the display is "spectacular" (20). But this is achieved through the government's intervention, and the result is diminished in his eyes by the fact that the people have no choice in the matter. Citizens have lost the control they once had over their lives.

The narrator does admit that the fireworks show is "splendid" (23), but in his jaded view he notes that some of the display is composed of genuine "emeralds," but regrets much of it is in the form of "zircons" (25), fake diamonds. This symbolizes his frustration with the government's ever-increasing intrusion into our lives. The emeralds represent the positive aspects of government which are truly fair, reasonable, and beneficial for the people. But the zircons, which flower "as they fall" (26), depict the oppressive nature of authority. The "noise of thunder" (27) heard "distantly" (27) is the rumbling of discontent brewing among the citizens but with insufficient strength to create change. The government will continue on the path it has set for itself.

Crying with drunken, "happy tears" (28), the narrator calls to God to "bless our Nation on a night like this" (29). He is torn between the love he feels for this land and the sorrow he experiences when he recognizes that we are rapidly moving away from the "blessings of liberty" espoused by the Founding Fathers. It seems that the alcohol the narrator has consumed, far from clouding and distorting his vision, has given him a new insight into this country's political being. Like his "half-afloat" (28) eyes, he believes the nation is slowly sinking as it drowns in a sea of restrictions, laws, codes and rules, with every aspect of daily life regulated and legislated.

The final two lines of the poem ask God to "bless the careful and secure officials/Who celebrate our independence now" (30–31). Slowly but surely the people have relinquished much of their freedom to government bureaucracy, but the full irony of the poem is contained in the revelation that on the Fourth of July, the day to celebrate America's freedom, that celebration is in a form dictated by the government. We have come a long way from Jefferson's premise "that government is best which governs least."

Works Cited

Nemerov, Howard. "The Fourth of July." *The Bedford Introduction to Literature*. Ed. Michael Meyer. 3rd ed. Boston: Bedford—St. Martin's, 1993. 705–706.

Beekeeping Imagery in "Stings" and "The Bee God"

Faraa Mobini

*Assignment: In this out-of-class assignment, the
student was asked to build on class discussion by
comparing and contrasting a poem by Ted Hughes
and one by Sylvia Plath.*

Marriage is an emotional, physical, and intellectual union
between two people. The couple has to put forth effort in the
marriage in order to sustain a long-lasting, manageable, and lively
marriage; otherwise, it will eventually deteriorate. In the typical
ending of many fairy tales, a dashing young man and a beautiful
young woman marry, have children, and live happily ever after.
Unfortunately, such a scenario is more common in fairy tales than
in real life. An example of a failing marriage and its psychological
effects on the married couple can be observed in the marriage of
poets Sylvia Plath and Ted Hughes. Their marriage slowly came
to an end: Plath wanted revenge and Hughes wanted distance. In
their poems "Stings" and "The Bee God," one can see, through the
beekeeping imagery, the roles each played in their deteriorating
relationship.

Plath characterizes herself and her declining role in her
marriage in "Stings." The poem begins with Plath observing a beehive in which she is looking for the queen bee. Plath questions the
existence of the queen bee by asking, "Is there any queen at all in

it?" (15). Plath goes on to describe what the queen bee would look like if she did exist:

> If there is, she is old,
> Her wings torn shawls, her long body
> Rubbed of its plush—
> Poor and bare and unqueenly and even shameful. (16–19)

The queen bee symbolizes a useless woman who has completed her task as a bearer of children and who is being replaced with another. This idea is implied when she says, "I stand in a column/ of winged unmiraculous women" (20–21). Plath sees herself as a part of the bee community, and she takes on the persona of a queen bee, whose life is coming to an end; she, like the aging queen bee, feels worthless. When Plath realizes that her life with her husband is ending, she says:

> It is almost over.
> I am in control.
> Here is my honey-machine,
> It will work without thinking,
> Opening, in spring, like an industrious virgin. (31–35)

Hughes' life will continue to prosper without Plath, just as the hive will continue to cycle when the queen bee departs. Plath feels like a discarded queen bee, not only being replaced, but also being thrown out of the hive to wither away and die.

Hughes in "The Bee God" also sees Plath as being in-tune with the bee colony. Hughes personifies Plath by saying, "So you became the Abbess/ In the nunnery of the bees" (5–6). Plath's father, Otto Plath, is portrayed as the Bee God of the colony, and Plath is the chief worshipper in service to him and his bees. Beekeeping originates as a hobby for Plath to take her mind off of her stress and her worries; however, it eventually becomes her obsession. Hughes shows this obsession when he says, "But you bowed over your bees/ As you bowed over your Daddy" (13–14). Beekeeping allows Plath to reconnect with her father's memory, causing Hughes to feel like an outsider, a stranger to the bee colony. Therefore, while "Stings" personifies Plath as a queen bee falling out of her destiny and being thrown out of her colony, "The Bee God" personifies Plath as an Abbess to her father, which, in turn, causes her own decline.

Not only does Plath in her poem characterize herself and portray her role in her marriage to Hughes, but she also goes on to portray Hughes' role in their deteriorating marriage. While Plath carries out her bee-keeping tasks, she mentions Hughes observing her actions. In her poem, "Stings," Plath says, "A third person is watching. / He has nothing to do with the bee-seller or with me. / Now he is gone" (39–41). Plath does not consider Hughes as a part of the bee colony, and she feels that he has nothing to do with the raising of the bees. Hughes is an exile figure who has been discarded by Plath. Nevertheless, at one point in the poem, Plath does go on to say, "He was sweet" (45). This statement implies that Hughes is the flower outside of the bee colony. He is sweet like the flower is to a bee, only temporarily, until the sweetness vanishes and another flower needs to be discovered. When the sweetness has disappeared, the flower deserts Plath, and she is left isolated, alone in the bee colony. Plath views Hughes as distant, not a part of the bee colony.

In "The Bee God," Hughes also characterizes himself as distant. "The Bee God" opens, saying, "When you wanted bees I never dreamed / It meant your daddy had come up out of the well" (1–2). Hughes goes on to say, "I scoured the old hive, you painted it, / White, with crimson hearts and flowers, and bluebirds" (3–4). Hughes offers Plath the beehives as an opportunity for tranquility, peace, and happiness in their lives. In return, Plath shuts Hughes out of her life and distances herself from him. Plath becomes obsessed with the bees. Hughes says, "You did not want me to go but your bees had their own ideas. / You wanted the honey, you wanted those big blossoms / Clotted like first milk, and the fruit like babies" (23–25). Hughes senses that Plath is separating herself from him, but he also sees a sympathetic side of her that wants to hold onto him. Eventually, she manages to push him away. Hughes personifies this stinging action when he says:

> The outrider tangled, struggled, stung—
> Marking the target.
> And I was flung like a headshot jackrabbit
> Through sunlit whizzing tracers
> As bees planted their volts, their thudding electrodes,
> In on their target. (31–36)

Plath is personified as the bee who stings Hughes and pushes him away, distancing him and causing him to leave her alone to her own satisfaction.

While Hughes thinks the hobby of beekeeping will keep Plath's mind off of suicidal thoughts and help revitalize her, the activity actually makes her more distant and destroys the marriage even more. Plath realizes that the marriage is not working, and Hughes realizes that Plath is more mentally ill than she appears. Hughes' love for Plath causes him to wipe out her imperfections, but now he is beginning to see her weaknesses and her insanity. In "Stings," Plath waves a final farewell to Hughes. Plath considers death as her final departure from Hughes when she says:

> They thought death was worth it, but I
> Have a self to recover, a queen.
> Is she dead, is she sleeping?
> Where has she been,
> With her lion-red body, her wings of glass? (51–55)

Plath contemplates a moment of despair as she is falling and as she realizes her marriage is deteriorating; however, she bounces back on her feet and says, in effect, "No I won't go down like this!" Plath describes her revitalized spirit by saying:

> Now she is flying
> More terrible than she ever was, red
> Scar in the sky, red comet
> Over the engine that killed her—
> The mausoleum, the wax house. (56–60)

Plath becomes more powerful after her marriage. In her marriage, she lost herself; her home and domestic situation had killed her, but she survived. Now, she is coming back to get revenge. Plath has a rage to survive: either fight for her way back or fight her way through. Plath envisions Hughes as a beehive that steals her youth, and now that she is free of him, she will get revenge. She is going to rise—determined, strong, willful, and vengeful; she is not going to let anything defeat her.

Although Plath blames Hughes for wasting her youth, Hughes feels things happen for a reason and that the two of them are just not meant to be together. Hughes lets go of the marriage because he feels as though he cannot be of any assistance to Plath and that she is already doomed. After Hughes is stung by the bees, he closes out his poem, "The Bee God," by saying, "Who came-Fanatics for their God, the God of the Bees, / Deaf to your pleas as the fixed stars—/At the bottom of the well" (47–49). Plath's love for her father is too strong, and she cannot rid herself of this obsession. Her love for her father is much stronger than the bond she has with Hughes; Plath is permitting the bees and her father to deteriorate and kill not only her, but also her marriage. The fixed stars at the bottom of the well symbolize the couples' destiny and the fact that they cannot escape it; they have to accept the termination of their marriage. The bees interfere with their relationship, and Plath's relationship with her father overcomes her marriage with Hughes, causing her to jump back into depression. Hughes blames Otto Plath for Plath's depression, and Plath blames Hughes.

In her poem, "Stings," Plath speaks through a misshapen mouth of bitterness. Her poetry is in the language of mortal illness. Hughes, on the other hand, plainly narrates his relationship with Plath and even manages to write in the same manner as Plath herself by employing the same bee imagery, with deftness and poignancy. The bee imagery symbolizes life, the life of Plath and Hughes together coming to an end. Both Plath and Hughes use bee imagery to show that their deteriorating marriage is over like a queen bee's functions are over at some point. The bee community has to start over with a new queen bee, and Hughes feels he also needs to find a new queen bee because Plath's job is over. Plath refuses to accept that her life is ending; instead, she insists on fighting back and getting revenge on Hughes for taking her youth and her life. After all, Hughes leaves Plath alone, angry, and depressed. Hughes' cruelty eventually drives Plath's delicate soul to take her own life. So who is to blame for the deteriorating marriage? Plath blames Hughes for stealing her youth and taking her life away from her and then deserting her. Hughes blames Plath because she is overly obsessed with her father and is slowly crumbling inside; he says that he has no other choice but to leave her. In a way, they are both to blame for giving up faith in each other and losing respect for one another. Exactly why did Hughes give up on the marriage so easily? And why was Plath determined to destroy Hughes? Perhaps, Plath and Hughes are more concerned about their individual success in life rather than improving the quality of their lives together as a whole, as one unity. In a marriage, the couple is either unified or the marriage is worthless.

Works Cited

Hughes, Ted. "The Bee God." *Birthday Letters*. New York: Farrar Straus Giroux, 1998. 150–152.

Plath, Sylvia. "Stings." *Ariel*. New York: HarperPerennial, 1999. 69–71.

A Reading of Gender in Othello

Marcia Justice

Assignment: In this out-of-class essay, the student was to analyze the male character's feelings about women in general in Shakespeare's Othello and to explore how their thoughts on the subject of women contribute to the overall theme of the play.

William Shakespeare's play Othello is ostensibly about the heroic warrior Othello, of Moor descent, who is an expatriate general of some high reputation and respect in Venetian society despite his minority status. His nemesis turns out to be Iago, Othello's "Ancient" who has loyally served with Othello through many battles but who now harbors some deep grudges against Othello even while he continues to profess his love for and undying service to the General. In essence, however, the play is not only about Othello and Iago at odds with one another but also about men's pride in general; Othello is permeated with jealousy, envy, misogyny, racism, deceit, betrayal, and false professions of love and honesty, all of which are spawned from the self-absorptions exhibited by its male players. All of these destructive views and emotions are borne from the myopic preoccupations these men have with themselves. Othello thus offers an intriguing exploration of these men's "pride and purposes" (1.1.12).

The play opens with Othello's elopement with a Venetian Senator's daughter, Desdemona. She is the opposite of Othello in every way. She is white, and he is black. She has been sheltered and gently raised, while he has been sold into slavery and has battled for his survival. She is young and naïve, while he is older and worldly. She is his prize, his spoils--and he revels in his conquest. Despite his flowery professions, it is doubtful that Othello actually loves Desdemona: he loves the idea of her being in his possession. Desdemona, on the other hand, exhibits a deep faith and love in Othello throughout the play, even trying to protect him as she lies dying at Othello's hand and is asked by Emilia who has killed her: "Nobody—I myself. Farewell. / Commend me to my kind Lord" (5.2.125–126).

In contrast, Othello exhibits no faith, warmth or true emotion for Desdemona. What he does express is an appreciation for her adoration of him when they first meet: "She loved me for the dangers I had passed, / And I loved her that she did pity them" (1.3.167–168). Othello does not care enough for her, however, to ask for her father's approval or wait for a public wedding, opting instead to elope in the middle of the night. When he believes his reputation will be impugned in any way by her real or imaged actions, he is willing to take her life. A fascinating line is uttered by Othello when he is preparing to kill his wife: "Yet she must die, else she'll betray more men" (5.2.6). Obviously, she is less important to him even than the betrayal of men in general. Why? Because the only thing that truly matters to Othello is his pride in how he is held in esteem by other men.

This pride is further emphasized with Othello's self-aggrandizement when, near the end of the play, he has killed Desdemona and now realizes that instead of being lauded by other men for defending his "honor", he will instead lose his standing among them. He selects to kill himself, but not before calling Gratiano into the room to witness his last oration in which Othello tries to ensure a legacy that he was an honorable man and legendary solder. He calls himself, "An honorable murderer" (5.2.295) and says, "I have done the state some service, and they know't" (5.2.229). He also makes a last pitch for remembrance of his military heroics:

> I have seen the day
> That with this little arm and this good sword
> I have made my way through more impediments
> Than twenty times your stop." (5.2.262-265)

Othello is not mourning for Desdemona: he is busy thinking of himself and asking Gratiano to ensure that the world remembers what a great man and soldier Othello has been.

The supporting male characters in this play exhibit this same trait. When Desdemona's father, Brabantino, is advised of his daughter's midnight elopement, he does not express concern about his daughter's welfare, demand annulment, or take any responsibility for leaving his young daughter exposed to Othello's influence. Othello states "Her father loved me, oft invited me; / Still questioned me the story of my life / From year to year" (1.3.128–130). The Duke of Venice even seems to chide Brabantino for this stating, "I think this tale would win my daughter too" (1.3.171). Instead Brabantino blames witchcraft and then the deceitfulness of his daughter's nature, both of which are false conjectures. He goes so far as to besmirch his daughter to her new husband in order to keep his pride intact: "She has deceived her father, and may thee" (1.3.292).

Rodrigo and Cassio also center their behaviors on prideful egos. Rodrigo professes undying love for Desdemona, but he wants to soothe his pride over her rejection of him for the Moor so badly that he appears willing to stoop to any level to barter with Iago for a way to simply satisfy his lust for her. While Cassio knows Bianca is a prostitute, he nevertheless takes advantage of her affections and then ridicules her to other males in order to maintain their approval of him.

Iago, though, is perhaps the most egocentric of all the male characters. He definitely considers himself to be the smartest of them all, the master manipulator who is above being found out. He believes himself to be supremely justified in whatever he does, whether seeking to claim the Lieutenant position by ruining Cassio's reputation or by causing irreversible damage to Othello's marriage:

> Till I am evened with him, wife for wife;
> Or failing so, yet that I put the Moor
> At least into a jealousy so strong
> That judgment cannot cure." (2.1.275–279)

Iago does not have any concern for Desdemona's welfare in this process—or anyone else's. He considers any casualties justifiable for his causes. He kills Rodrigo to protect himself, yet earlier in the play he states, "Though in the trade of war I have slain men, / Yet do I hold it very stuff o' th' conscience / To do no contrived murther" (1.2.1–3). While he declares himself "honest" in every scene, he is deceitful in all of his endeavors, even with his wife

Emilia. Further, he publicly speaks badly of her and women in general and considers himself amusing for doing so. He is greatly concerned, however, with his stature among other men, which is why he is so obsessed with obtaining the Lieutenant position and maintaining his intimate association with Othello, right up to the very end. He will not simply quit Othello's service: "I follow him to serve my turn upon him"(1.1.42), he states to Rodrigo. He has too much pride to be outdone by a Moor.

Each of these men is indifferent to anything but his self-importance. The women in *Othello* know this fact, accept it, and are resigned to it in a disturbing way. Desdemona implies excusal of such behavior in "The Willow Song" when she sings, "Let nobody blame him; his scorn I approve" (4.3.50). But Emilia voices the most lucid view of these men:

> 'Tis not a year or two shows us a man.
> They are all but stomachs, and we all but food;
> They eat us hungerly, and when they are full,
> They belch us." (3.4.98–101)

While Emilia is speaking of the men's way of dealing with their women, destroying any true love and commitment by their prideful self-centeredness, hers is also an astute observation of how these men, in the end, also destroy themselves.

Works Cited

Shakespeare, William. *Othello: the Moor of Venice. The Compact Bedford Introduction to Literature.* Ed. Michael Meyer. 7th ed. New York: Bedford—St. Martin's Press, 2005. 1037–1117.

Idealist versus Escapist: Contrasting Worldviews in The Glass Menagerie

Melissa Miller

Assignment: In this out-of-class essay, the student was to compare how Williams portrays the world views of Jim and Laura

In his 1945 play, *The Glass Menagerie*, playwright Tennessee Williams exposes the plights of desperate Americans during the Great Depression and the public response to this ordeal. In this era, economic instability transformed America from a country of prosperity and wealth into a nation of disillusionment and slain hopes, plunging the unsuspecting America into the draconian realities of unemployment, poverty, and hunger. Even as American tenacity weakened, however, men and women tried to disregard the bleakness of this economic and social crisis with dreams of grandeur and goals of wealth, hoping to create a "rags to riches" effect. In his play, Williams unmasks this reaction to the Great Depression through the character Jim O'Connor and shows a counter-reaction through the character Laura Wingfield. While Jim is shown to be an inflated dreamer, Laura is described as a frail "home girl," devoid of aspirations, who finds solace and security in her alternate world of transparent glass (453). In this disclosure, Williams illuminates Jim's and Laura's opposing worldviews during the bleak 1930s

America, demonstrating that in this time of despair, the worldly Jim subscribes to blind optimism while the escapist Laura tries to evade reality.

In the play, narrator Tom describes Jim as an ambitious ideal-ist whose high school glory has faded into a mediocre job with mod-est recognition. Throughout his life, Jim has strived to become an accomplished person, but because of unspecified "interference," he now works in a factory as a shipping clerk for a substandard wage (461). His current position as a struggling underdog is in direct contrast with the brilliance of his teenage years. In high school, Jim was, as Tom says, a "hero" moving "in a continual spotlight" (460). His fall from greatness following graduation has left Jim hungry for the glory he once enjoyed. As a result, he has subscribed to the philosophy of self-improvement, seeking to compensate for his years of failure and disappointment. In accordance with his philosophy, he defines success simply as "knowledge," "money," and "power" (476). Because of this definition, he measures himself and his future success based on the acquisition of these ideals. He tries to improve his adverse circumstances with confidence and optimism. As Roger B. Stein suggests, "To Jim the warehouse is not a prison but a rung on the ladder toward success." During his visit with the Wingfield family, Jim tries to indoctrinate Laura with this psychology: "You don't have the proper amount of faith in yourself" (475). Jim tries to explain to her the elements of success as 1930s America defined them. Jim sums up his worldview when he arrogantly tells Laura, "Think of yourself as *superior* in some way" (476). Like many others in this era, Jim believes that, in order to prosper, he must consider himself better than others, regardless of reality. In Jim, Williams reveals the blind, callous perspective of pushy, self-absorbed Amer-icans during the Great Depression.

As the antithesis of Jim, Laura lives in a world of isolation and imagination rather than one of interaction and reality. In contrast to Jim's confident rants on self-improvement and superiority, the timid, fragile Laura imparts to the gentleman caller her primary interest in life: the glass collection. When Jim asks what captivates her, the recluse stammers, "Well, I do—as I said—have my—glass collection" (476). With limited contact from the world outside the Wingfield apartment, she spends her days trapped in a world of transparent glass, shielded from reality. During her conversation with Jim, the "emissary from a world of reality," she introduces him to her favorite glass figurine, the unicorn (439). She cautions Jim as he holds the mythical animal, saying, "Oh, be careful—if you breathe, it breaks!" (476). When Laura says this, she indicates that the glass unicorn is exceedingly fragile and will break with only slight agitation. She not only reveals her likeness to the cherished figurine, but also that her well being at this point lies with Jim. In this, he is representative of the outside world because with the slightest upset, this world will break Laura if she ventures into public, as it did in the business college fiasco earlier in the play. Through her description of the nature of the glass menagerie, she outlines her perspective on the world: "Glass breaks so easily. No matter how careful you are" (478). In this statement, Laura expresses her view that incredibly fragile people are bound to break at the first sign of adversity in the real world. She also knows that she herself is prone to fracture and that she is incapable of coping with the hostile world outside of her apartment. Thus, she confines herself to her alternate reality, further alienating herself from the callous, goal-oriented America of this time period.

The battling perspectives of callous, self-centered American industriousness versus a retreat from reality form an underlying conflict in Tennessee Williams's play, *The Glass Menagerie*. By contrasting the responses of two characters, Jim and Laura, Williams posits that ordeal will elicit varying reactions from people of diverse worldviews. While Jim holds the idea that knowledge and power are the keys to success for himself and for everyone, Laura instead feels that people who travel into the cold world from which she is isolated are doomed to break.

Works Cited

Stein, Roger B. "'The Glass Menagerie' Revisited: Catastrophe without Violence." *Western Humanities Review*. 28.2 (1964): 141–153. *Literature Resource Center*. Gale Group Databases. Macon State College Library, Macon, GA. 13 March 2006 <http://galenet.galegroup.com/servlet/LitRC?locID=maco12153>.

Williams, Tennessee. *The Glass Menagerie*. Making Literature Matter: An Anthology for Readers and Writers. Ed. John Schilb and John Clifford. 2nd ed. Boston: Bedford/St. Martin's, 2003. 437–483.

Character and Purpose in A Doll's House *and* Fences

Clint Adams

Assignment: In this out-of-class essay, the student was to analyze assigned works of drama.

A Doll's House and *Fences* are both plays dealing with the human consequences of social injustice. They are of comparable length, and each takes place in a confined setting. The pieces can then be said to be very similar, but I propose that they differ in at least one key aspect: characterization. In *A Doll's House*, Henrik Ibsen seems so thoroughly consumed by his message that he creates characters that are almost sketches. The characters in August Wilson's *Fences* are in stark contrast. They appear fleshed out and fully human; they are whole. This difference can be most clearly illustrated through a contrast of both the main characters (Torvald with Troy and Nora with Rose) and the ancillary characters in each piece.

First, there is the contrast between Torvald and Troy. Both are, to a certain degree, victims of the society in which they live. The prevailing ideas of Torvald's day regarding the respective roles of men and women leave him close-minded and incapable of understanding his wife. The prejudice and cruelty that Troy experiences in his youth forever skew the way he sees the world, leaving him frozen into a world view that cannot acknowledge changing times. The difference is that the reader is allowed to see Troy's exposure to the influences that damage him. Torvald's actions are presented with no real context. So, whereas Troy comes off as a misguided character, Torvald seems almost monstrous. The reader is able to take into consideration the abuses Troy suffered as a child and as a young man when evaluating his callous behavior to his wife and sons. With Torvald, no such mitigating factors are presented, leaving him seeming almost disgusting as he rages against the woman who put herself in danger to save his very life and never sought any remuneration. Troy seems human, possessing all the frailties that come with that distinction; Torvald seems less than that.

One can also see a contrast between Nora and Rose, though it is not of exactly the same kind. Once again, the two have fundamental similarities. They are both, at least initially, very much in love with their husbands; they are both forced to face a great flaw in these men; and they are both, to a certain degree, changed by this experience. The differences can be seen in the manner in which they change and the type of change they enact. Nora seems to undergo an immense metamorphosis in what is practically no time at all. For the vast majority of the play she is childlike, the doll in *A Doll's House*. She, by her own account, is little more than an amusing plaything for Torvald. Then, in the final scene, she is transformed in an instant by Torvald's cold indifference to her sacrifice. She makes the transition from puppet to fully emancipated woman in the blink of an eye, turning her back on the man she was nearly fully dependent on and seeking to find her own true self. The change was in her best interest and makes a strong social statement, but in its incredible manner it damages the realism of the piece. With Rose, the situation is quite different. For one thing, the reader is allowed to see her and Troy's relationship over a period of years, as opposed to the mere days glimpsed between Nora and Torvald. This greater span gives a more concrete and detailed impression of the inner workings of the couple's relationship. Troy's demons and the so-called "fences" that they build between him and Rose, among others, are spread out and displayed clearly. This facilitates a greater understanding of her reaction. The reader is allowed to grasp the full force of the betrayal she must feel in learning that Troy has been unfaithful to her after she has put her heart and soul into their relationship for nearly two decades. Also, her reaction is more in harmony with average expectations. She stays with Troy for the sake of Raynell, but informs him that he is a "womanless man" (1133).

In this manner, the painful consequences of Troy's failings are illustrated without violating the realism of the story.

The final contrast between the plays is in the utilization of ancillary characters. As before, parallels are evident. Each play contains three children. Both have a character that holds the position of best friend of the male protagonist. However, the way in which secondary characters are used in the two plays could not be more different. In *A Doll's House*, if the main characters seem like sketches, then the secondary ones seem almost like tools. The children are complete non-entities. With the exception of Nora's avoidance of them after Torvald's speech on how deceit corrupts children, they have no discernable presence in the play. Dr. Rank seems to be there only to emphasize Nora's compassion and Torvald's coldness. Krogstad and Kristine serve to advance the plot and to contrast the relationship of Torvald and Nora. There is no in-depth understanding of these characters. They seem like almost a part of the setting more than people. In *Fences*, the opposite seems to be true. The personality of every character is developed compellingly. One can get inside the minds of all of the secondary characters. They are not just objects to affect the main characters and be affected by them. Lyons and Cory are not merely sympathetic creations showcasing their father's failures in parenting; they are people possessing good and bad elements, some inherited from Troy and some of their own making. Bono is a kind, gentle soul who sees the goodness that is in Troy and tries, throughout the play, to protect him from his lower impulses. Gabriel is a truly tragic figure and acts as the fool speaking wisdom. Even Raynell, short as her portion of dialogue is, possesses a unique personality: a sort of innocent naiveté. Through her words, Cory is reconciled to his father in death, and the reader is allowed to see Troy for what he was: just a man, struggling like all others. So, whereas Ibsen's characters work for the plot, Wilson's exist for the reader.

In essence then, the thing that seems most to separate *A Doll's House* and *Fences* is their focus. *A Doll's House* was conceived with the specific purpose of conveying a message about the way society operated. Ibsen even once said in one of his letters that the whole of the play was merely designed to lead up to the last climactic scene and Nora's famous lines. The focus in *Fences* appears to have been first to tell a story, to paint a picture. The picture created says certain things and has certain implications, but it is an entity to itself. It does not lead to something great; it is something great.

Works Cited

Ibsen, Henrik. *A Doll's House. Literature for Composition.* Ed. Sylvan Barnet et al. 5th ed. New York: Longman, 2000. 774–824.

Wilson, August. *Fences. Literature for Composition.* Ed. Sylvan Barnet et al. 5th ed. New York: Longman, 2000. 1096–1143.

Light into Darkness

Lamar Tipton

Assignment: In this paper planned outside of class and completed in class, the student was asked to examine characterization in Shakespeare's Macbeth.

William Shakespeare's *Macbeth* is the tragic drama of a courageous and powerful man who brings about his own destruction. By all appearances Macbeth is destined for greatness. However, appearances can be deceiving. Alas, his future would not follow the natural progression of things set forth throughout a lifetime of blood, sweat, and honorable deeds. Lack of self-control is Macbeth's tragic flaw. In the end his "vaulting ambition" (1.7.27), his absurd rashness, and his tumultuous impatience are the ranking culprits of his ruin.

To appreciate fully the complete and utter devastation which Macbeth brings upon himself, it is critical to take full measure of his life during the days and weeks preceding his infamous crime. During this period, Macbeth's future appears fruitful and bursting with promise. He is a man of high regard and a national hero. He has won the respect and admiration of king and country. He is rewarded by his king for heroic victory in bloody battle. King Duncan names Macbeth the Thane of Cawdor and reveals his further indebtedness to his beloved kinsman with the words "More is thy due than more than all can pay" (1.4.21). The name of Macbeth seems destined to cross the lips of generations as they sing of his great deeds. He should grow old in proud retrospection of past achievements,

warmly surrounded by friends and admirers. All of this awaits
Macbeth if he can still his murderous desire for the throne. All such
promise dissolves in a mixture of blood, fear, and haunted conscience upon the merciless point of the groomsman's blade.

The ill-conceived plot to drug the groomsmen and to use their
knives to murder the sleeping Duncan is the beginning of the end
for Macbeth. In their impetuous haste "to catch the nearest way"
(1.5.18), he and Lady Macbeth throw caution and sound reason to
the wind. It is clear that at this point Macbeth can no longer control his lustful ambition. After all, Duncan is thrice charmed at
Inverness. He is king, kinsman, and guest. Macbeth is also fully
aware of the physical, mental, and spiritual consequences even
before the murder takes place. For instance, he knows that he will
carry in his heart the eternal fear of "even handed justice" (1.7.10).
He is also concerned that this crime could "jump the life to come"
(1.7.7), thereby extinguishing all hope for the afterlife. Under the
threat of such grave retribution, it would seem that nothing could
convince a rational thinking Macbeth to follow through with this
homicidal nightmare.

There is great hope as Macbeth steels himself to reason in
what might well be the final lucid moment of his life. His last few
honorable breaths bring forth the following words:

> "We will proceed no further in this business;
> He hath honor'd me of late, and I have bought
> Golden opinions from all sorts of people,
> Which would be worn now in their newest gloss,
> Not cast aside so soon." (1.7.32–36)

At this moment above all others his life hangs in the balance. That
the scales are so easily tipped by Lady Macbeth's taunts concerning
his manhood is evidence of his inability to control his straying
thoughts. Proper self-control would elicit fresh images of past con-
quests to thwart such nonsense, had Macbeth so desired. Lady
Macbeth is able to prompt her husband to commit murder, with
cliché lines such as "From this time / Such I account thy love"
(1.7.39–40) and the previously mentioned taunts of cowardice. It is
certain that Macbeth's weak grasp on his own voracious ambition
provides his wife with easy prey for manipulation.

Macbeth craves the crown to the extent that reason is beyond
his grasp. In Macbeth's tortured mind, rashness replaces rational

thought as if each moment endured in the absence of his all-consuming goal is torture. Nothing else matters. He willingly sacrifices all in a solitary defining instant. In one wild and craven moment of bloodletting horror, Macbeth kills Duncan, and in effect he kills himself.

Works Cited

Shakespeare, William. *The Tragedy of Macbeth*. Ed. E. M. Waith. Rev. ed. New Haven: Yale University Press, 1963.

Multiple Conflicts

Lauren Herbert

Assignment: In this out-of-class essay, the student was asked to develop a character analysis of Willy Loman in Death of a Salesman.

Throughout a man's life, there are many goals and expectations that go beyond the present. Many wish to be a better person some-day and hope to make the best situation for loved ones. Others have the desire to test their boundaries and explore their world. More often than not, the dream of many men is to have a good job with a loving wife and children who respect them. Although all of these are noble goals, no one goal is the best for every individual to strive for. No matter what they choose to do in their lives, they will always wonder if past decisions will influence their lives. Unlike the desired situa-tion, Arthur Miller shows Willy Loman in *Death of a Salesman* as a man in conflict with his setting, his sons, and himself.

As Miller uses the setting of the play as an antagonist, Willy is not happy with his surroundings at all. The apartment buildings that have been built next to his house show how his life is closing in on him. He feels closed off from the rest of the world. There is no yard or "fresh air" (1671) for Willy to feel as though he is in the same house which he bought years ago. He can not plant a garden or have anything grow because of the "bricks and windows, win-dows and bricks" (1671) that block the sunlight from his little bit of yard. The buildings are so close together and the walls so thin that conversations can be heard from one room to another, or one house to another. On a closer level, his house and appliances are falling apart. Willy puts a new ceiling in one room which shows a form of closing-in as a part of his everyday life. Despite the fact that some appliances are not paid for, they are falling apart. With only one payment left, the refrigerator "just broke again . . . it consumes belts" (1698). The shower "drips" (1695), and this shows how the simple tasks in life are getting difficult to handle.

Willy's sons offer another conflict as antagonists in the play. Because the boys and Willy never have a traditional father / son relationship, their individual relationships with each other suffer. He is not shown as a father figure but as a friend to his two sons. He does not discipline them as he would if he were more like a parent rather than a peer. He jokes and plays around with the boys as much as their friends. He is not around as they are growing up, and when he is around, it is for fun. As a traveling salesman, there is no time to build a lasting relationship with loved ones at home. Miller shows Willy's job in sales as a contributing factor in the unstable relationships with his sons. If Willy were not always away, Biff would not go to Boston and accidentally meet his father with the woman he is having an affair with. After this point, the tension between Biff and Willy gets so bad that Willy does not function the same way when Biff is around. From that point on, the father / son relationships are very hard on all involved.

Despite all else that is against Willy Loman, he has the biggest conflict within himself. Miller shows much of Willy's life through flashback. Unfortunately, these are flashbacks within the mind of the character and interfere with his normal functioning. Willy carries on conversations from years ago while speaking with someone in the present. He gets flashbacks of his affair and of his brother, and these experiences make Willy see how inadequate his life is now in the present. He remembers that he could have gone with Ben, his brother, to foreign lands to make something of himself. Linda's influence, however, makes Willy stay and think he will succeed as a traveling salesman. Willy learns some new information about his dead father from the flashbacks with his brother. When the flashbacks of the affair come to Willy, he realizes that Biff would have been something and somebody if he had not witnessed that event. The affair is what tears Biff's life apart, and therefore Willy's life.

Willy Loman is shown as a man with many problems in the play. He wants to enjoy life, but he has put too many expectations on his sons and what he could make of his life. As he sets his goals too high, he is constantly faced with disappointment. Although he is constantly traveling and meeting new people, Willy is not happy with his life as a traveling salesman and is missing many of the important changes that go on in his loved ones' lives. He is dealing internally with what he could have done but chose not to. The character of Willy Loman shows how people should not let life go by without some sort of change and diversity within it. A life that is extremely monotonous is bound to make one miserable and too set in the norm to desire change.

Works Cited

Miller, Arthur. *Death of a Salesman. The Bedford Introduction to Literature.* Ed. Michael Meyer. 4th ed. New York—St. Martin's Press, 1996. 1668–1731.

The Use of Symbolism in Character Development in The Glass Menagerie

Stephen Travis Yates

Assignment: In this out-of-class assignment, the student was to discuss a specific element in an assigned play.

In *The Glass Menagerie*, by Tennessee Williams, the use of symbolism contributes to the development of character. Tom Wingfield is a character who has tremendous hopes and dreams, but he is unable to achieve them while remaining in his prison-like home. It is through the effective use of symbolism that the reader is able to understand the complexity and importance of Tom's aspirations. However, this use of symbolism also reveals that his dreams will never be fulfilled.

Tom lives in a world in which he feels trapped. Williams characterizes him as a "poet with a job in a warehouse" (1624). This statement is very important because it contrasts the creativity of Tom with the uncreative and banal world in which he lives. Tom does have hope of becoming a poet, but his outlook on such a future is bleak. After Tom witnesses a magic show, he tells his sister Laura that "the wonderfullest trick of all was the coffin trick" (Williams 1635). He tells her that the magician "got out of the coffin without removing one nail" (Williams 1635). The references to the coffin reveal Tom's character and his view of his own numbed life. Tom pictures himself as a restricted and dead individual in a "2 by 4 situation" (Williams 1635), but he hopes that one day his dreams will come true and he can escape from his depressing surroundings. Tom manages to find temporary comfort as he "plunges out on the fire escape" (Williams 1666). The fire escape is a symbol used frequently throughout the play. It is more than a fire escape because it is a means by which Tom attempts to escape the confines of his apartment and the monotony of his everyday life. As Williams writes, the fire escape "is a touch of accidental poetic truth, for all of those huge buildings are always burning with the slow and implacable fires of human desperation" (1865).

In order to accomplish his goals, Tom realizes he must leave his current environment, even if it requires abandoning his mother and sister. He wants more out of life, and he desires a "future that doesn't include the warehouse" (Williams 1650). It is through the use of symbolism that Tom's hopes can be shown in full detail. In describing to Laura the performance of Malvolio the Magician, he tells her that goldfish were made to "fly away canaries" (Williams 1635). Like the canaries, Tom hopes one day to escape the imprisonment of his cage-like home. Throughout the play, these hopes are conveyed through symbolic rainbows. Tom receives from the magician a "shimmering rainbow-colored scarf" (Williams 1635). As Tom views the Paradise Dance Hall from his apartment, he sees "a large glass sphere that hung from the ceiling" (Williams 1641). In these symbolic rainbows, Tom is able to find hope, but he knows that, if his dreams of becoming a poet and restoring his life are to be fulfilled, he must truly escape from the drudgery of his present environment. As Tom wishes upon the symbolic "silver slipper of a moon" (Williams 1641), the reader is able to understand the incredible distance that Tom desires to escape from the world in which he lives.

It is when Tom finally leaves that he realizes that his hopes and dreams will never be fulfilled. After he symbolically "descended the steps of this fire escape for the last time" (Williams 1666) in an attempt to leave his past, he learns that his past can not be forgotten. He has met disappointment as he is constantly reminded of Laura, even though he tries "anything that can blow your candles out" (Williams 1666). As the rainbow was once used as a symbol of hope, it now becomes a symbol of broken and unfulfilled dreams.

While Tom is walking down the street, he passes a window "filled with pieces of colored glass, tiny transparent bottles in delicate colors, like bits of a shattered rainbow" (Williams 1666). Tom once possessed hopes for a more promising and happier future, but after he witnesses them become like a "shattered rainbow" (Williams 1666), he discovers that they will never be achieved.

Williams' play *The Glass Menagerie* is filled with symbolism that creates greater understanding of Tom's character by giving insight into his hopes and dreams. This symbolism shows the full strength and emotion of Tom's dreams, but it also reveals the sad fact that they will never come true.

Works Cited

Williams, Tennessee. *The Glass Menagerie. The Bedford Introduction to Literature.* Ed. Michael Meyer. 4th ed. Boston: Bedford—St. Martin's, 1996. 1624–1666.

Family Fences

Katrina Thrift

Assignment: In this out-of-class assignment, the student was to discuss a specific element in an assigned play.

In his play, *Fences*, August Wilson presents the reader with the harsh realities of a black family's struggle for sustaining life. Prejudice and disrespect are constant enemies for the black American of the time period. Wilson displays extraordinary talent in his ability to convey to the reader the barriers that present frustration for the Maxson family. He paints the picture of a man who becomes blind to his original vision of fighting discrimination. Through his defeat, he ultimately loses the people for whom he was originally fighting to provide a better life. Throughout his life, Troy Maxson finds himself as a man who is surrounded by fences, some of which serve as a means of containment and others which serve as barriers.

One physical fence is discussed by the characters during the play. It is the one which Rose has Troy build around the yard. The reader could consider that Rose has Troy build this fence in an attempt to contain him in the yard. Rose hopes it will serve as a reminder of what Troy has within that fence and possibly prevent his wandering. Yet Wilson doesn't allow Troy to finish this fence until closer to the end of Troy's life when he can no longer run. Troy's lack of determination to finish the fence reveals his effort to ensure an escape route from the world in which he lives. This fence is the only physical fence erected in the play. Yet Troy's frustration with the events in his life leads him to erect many other fences that serve as barriers to those closest to him.

The fence that Troy establishes with his close friend Jim Bono results from Troy's betrayal of his vow to strive to live the right kind of life. Troy and Bono's friendship developed during their time spent in the penitentiary. After their release, Bono admired the changed man that he felt that Troy had become. As time passes, however, Bono realizes that Troy is moving away from his revised values. During Bono's second discussion with Troy about Alberto, Bono tells Troy that he does not want to see him destroy the life that Troy has worked so hard to establish. Bono begins to view Troy as hypocritical. He tells Troy, "You's in control . . . that what you tell me all the time. You responsible for what you do" (1902). Troy builds this fence between them because Bono becomes the voice of a guilty conscience that Troy no longer wants to hear.

Troy also erects a fence in his relationship with Rose. Rose is an accepting but firm woman. However, she is unable to accept the fact that she has devoted eighteen years of her life to Troy, and in return he has chosen an extramarital affair. Troy's egoism shows as he tries to explain to Rose that he had to get away from their life. Rose has never allowed herself the same opportunity because she found herself fenced in by her devotion to Troy. She cannot accept the fact that he is no longer committed to her. Troy pleads with Rose that he has had to attempt to conquer all of the hardships that life has placed on him. In addition, he views himself as a failure because he has "been standing in the same place for eighteen years" (1906). Rose does not accept his excuses. Also, she reminds Troy that she has been standing right there with him. When Troy brings Raynell home for Rose to care for, she once again endures the evidence of Troy's adultery. However, Rose ensures that Troy is aware of the barrier he has constructed between them. Indeed, Rose assures Troy that this fence will never be removed: "I'll take care of your baby for you . . . cause . . . like you say . . . she's innocent . . . and you can't visit the sins of the father upon the child. A motherless child has got a hard time. From right now . . . this child got a mother. But you a womanless man" (1910).

Furthermore, there are fences that Troy has built in the relationships with his two sons. His older son, Lyons, represents a side of Troy that he does not want to acknowledge. Lyons is financially dependent on others in order to get by. He is unwilling to work for his dream to become an accomplished musician. Importantly, this financial dependence is also found in Troy's relationship with his brother Gabe. Troy got his start after his prison stay with the money received from Gabe. Troy tries to deny that he is actually taking advantage of Gabe. Instead, Troy tells himself that he is looking after Gabe's best interests. Troy's other son, Cory, is the person with whom Troy experiences the greatest conflict. Troy cannot control his jealousy of Cory's success as an athlete. The opportunities that are offered to Cory enrage Troy because they were available during Troy's time only to the white man. Instead of assisting his son in breaking down the fences he has had to climb over during his life, Troy builds the fences higher and stronger. He is selfishly determined that Cory will be denied any glory that might be achieved in his future football career. In addition, he denies Cory a greatly needed education that could lead him to a more secure future. As time passes, Cory becomes resentful that his father has created these barriers. Wilson shows Cory's rage in this statement to Troy. "You ain't never done nothing but hold me back. Afraid I was gonna do better than you" (1913). Troy is unable to handle the fact that Cory is aware of Troy's hypocritical ways. Therefore, Troy strengthens the wall between them as he forces his son to leave home. Cory lives with this barrier even after he leaves home and begins his new life. Cory returns home when Troy dies, but he feels that he is unable to attend the funeral. Rose tells Cory that he needs to put the past aside. Rose shares with her son, "Your daddy wanted you to be everything he wasn't . . . and at the same time he tried to make you into everything he was. I don't know if he was right or wrong . . . but I do know he meant to do more good than he meant to do harm" (1918). At this point, Cory has to decide if he is going to carry on the vicious tradition of building fences, or if he is strong enough to endure the change needed in order to break fences. Wilson makes it evident that Cory has chosen to break fences as he and Raynell evoke a good memory of their father as they begin to sing their father's song about the dog Blue.

The hardships that Troy suffers throughout his life are rooted in the discrimination that he experienced as a black man and from the destructive relationship that he had with his father. Yet it is his obduracy that leads him to erect fences between himself and those he loves best. The fences that Troy builds ironically represent the same type of barriers that he struggled to overcome during his earlier experiences in life.

Works Cited

Wilson, August. *Fences. The Bedford Introduction to Literature.* Ed. Michael Meyer. 3rd ed. Boston: Bedford—St. Martin's, 1993. 1872–1922.

The Two Lauras

Nancy Childs

Assignment: In this out-of-class essay, the student was to compare and contrast "Portrait of a Girl in Glass," a short story by Tennessee Williams, with his play, The Glass Menagerie.

Although "Portrait of a Girl in Glass" and *The Glass Menagerie* possess similar plots, Tennessee Williams elicits greater empathy for the characters in the play. He encourages the reader to empathize with their plight by focusing more detail on their personalities and individual struggles. Through Williams' skillful use of symbolism the reader gains a greater insight into Laura's struggle with her sense of inferiority and the resulting retreat into an imaginary world of glass.

In "Portrait of a Girl in Glass" Laura is portrayed as a lonely, detached young woman. Her brother, Tom, the narrator, describes her aloofness by saying, "she made no positive motion toward the world but stood at the edge of the water, so to speak, with feet that anticipated too much cold to move" (708). As Laura avoided the reality of her life and sought refuge in her bedroom, her world became one of "glass and also a world of music" (710). Her days were spent with her glass collection as "she washed and polished [them] with endless care" (709), and she often "sang to herself at night in her bedroom" (710) as she listened to old tunes on a 1920's Victrola. The story provides only a superficial picture of Laura's character, which does not reveal her need for an illusory world. The reader may feel sorry for this girl, but without an understanding of the reasons for her odd behavior, empathy is not evoked.

In the opening monologue of the play, the reader begins to understand the complexities of this family's life. Tom sets the scene by telling the reader, "I give you truth in the pleasant disguise of illusion" (1705). He describes Jim, the gentleman caller, as the "emissary from a world of reality that we were somehow set apart from" (1705). This statement immediately makes the reader aware of the fantasy world in which the Wingfields live. Tom suggests the sense of hopelessness the entire Wingfield family is attempting to evade as he uses Jim's character to symbolize "the long delayed but always expected something that we live for" (1705). They are out of touch with reality and live for a hope that seems to elude them. As Tom avoids the hopelessness through the adventure of the movies, Amanda escapes by living in the illusion of her past, and Laura retreats from the reality of her hopelessness through her glass menagerie.

As the play unfolds, the reader is given some possible explanations for the Wingfields' sense of hopelessness and despair. The father, who was "a telephone man who fell in love with long distances" (1706), has abandoned them. Tom is therefore denied his desire to be a poet and is confined to a warehouse job to support his mother and sister. Amanda is reduced from a life of advantage to a telephone subscriber's job and has no hope in sight of regaining the life she has lost. These same facts can be absorbed from the story. In the play, however, when Williams creates a life-controlling disability for Laura, the reader gains an understanding of the cause for her extreme inferiority complex. Laura reveals the impact of this disability when she tells Jim, "I had to go clumping all the way up the aisle with everyone watching!" (1740). Empathy is evoked as the reader senses Laura's self-consciousness and embarrassment because of her disability.

The descriptive detail assigned the glass ornaments that captivate Laura is not present in the story. These glass ornaments represent Laura's fragility and her unrealistic view of herself and her world. It is important to the reader's response that a glass unicorn is singled out for description. The parallel between a unicorn and Laura is significant. Just as the unicorn's horn makes him feel "freakish" (1745), Laura's clump makes her feel freakish. Just as the unicorn did not "feel at home with the other horses" (1745), Laura is uncomfortable in her world and just as fragile as this piece of glass. Her unrealistic view of her situation is revealed in her response to the unicorn's broken horn. She says, "I'll just imagine he had an operation" (1745), as if a simple operation could repair her problems. Williams uses this symbolism in the play to create empathy on the part of the reader for Laura's extreme sense of inferiority.

The two Lauras evoke differing responses. The reader may feel sorry for Laura in "Portrait of a Girl in Glass," but Williams elicits an empathetic response to her character in *The Glass Menagerie* through his use of symbolism. Her disability and the parallel between Laura and the unicorn help the reader to relate to her deep needs. Williams brings a depth to her character not realized in the story by providing the reader with insight into the reason for her retreat into the unrealistic world of glass.

Works Cited

Williams, Tennessee. "Portrait of a Girl in Glass." *Literature and Its Writers: An Introduction to Fiction, Poetry, and Drama.* Ed. Ann Charters and Samuel Charters. Boston: Bedford, 1997. 708–715.

———. *The Glass Menagerie. Literature and Its Writers: An Introduction to Fiction, Poetry, and Drama.* Ed. Ann Charters and Samuel Charters. Boston: Bedford, 1997. 1704–1750.